ESSENTIALS OF MARKETING
*General Editors:* D. W. SMALLBONE, BERNARD TAYLOR

# MARKETING AND THE SALES MANAGER

# MARKETING AND THE SALES MANAGER

BY

## FRANK H. ELSBY
*Ashridge Management College*

THE QUEEN'S AWARD
TO INDUSTRY 1966

PERGAMON PRESS
OXFORD · LONDON · EDINBURGH · NEW YORK
TORONTO · SYDNEY · PARIS · BRAUNSCHWEIG

PERGAMON PRESS LTD.,
Headington Hill Hall, Oxford
4 & 5 Fitzroy Square, London W.1
PERGAMON PRESS (SCOTLAND) LTD.,
2 & 3 Teviot Place, Edinburgh 1
PERGAMON PRESS INC.,
Maxwell House, Fairview Park, Elmsford, New York, 10523
PERGAMON OF CANADA LTD.,
207 Queen's Quay West, Toronto 1
PERGAMON PRESS (AUST.) PTY. LTD.,
19a Boundary Street, Rushcutters Bay, N.S.W. 2011, Australia
PERGAMON PRESS S.A.R.L.,
24 rue des Écoles, Paris 5e
VIEWEG & SOHN GMBH,
Burgplatz 1, Braunschweig

First edition 1969
Library of Congress Catalog Card No. 76–82910

*Printed in Great Britain by The European Printing Company, Bletchley, Bucks.*

08 006536 8 (flexicover)
08 006537 6 (hard cover)

# CONTENTS

# EDITORS' FOREWORD TO SERIES

THIS is a series of practical marketing handbooks written by British experts and designed as a library providing a compact and comprehensive review of modern marketing practice and technique.

The books are intended for sales and marketing managers, for marketing trainees and students of management, and for businessmen and managers of all kinds who are looking for an up-to-date, concise, readable statement of how the best British companies market their products.

Marketing as an accepted part of a business enterprise is a phenomenon of the last 10 years. Until then companies made goods and hoped that, by good fortune or through sales pressure, customers would be persuaded to buy them. As business has become more competitive, first in the consumer market and increasingly also in industrial markets, British managements have begun to appreciate the need for a rigorous and systematic approach to the market.

So much of the marketing approach seems obvious; it is surprising that the development of marketing thought and techniques should have spread so slowly through British industry. However, it is now possible to make a critical review of the best marketing practices in British industry. It is thus the purpose of this series to provide in simple terms descriptions and case studies demonstrating established techniques which can be used by the modern marketing executive to build for his company a strong position in the market and so make an important contribution to his company's profitability and contribute to the overall good of the community by ensuring that more and more people will be able to buy what they genuinely want and fewer customers will have to put up with second best.

The series has been so organized that, while each volume is self-contained, a connective thread runs through each so that the whole series will provide a compact and comprehensive review of marketing practice and techniques.

The editors would welcome at any time comments and criticism from their readers, and particularly suggestions for further additions to the range. The following titles are either available now or are in preparation:

*Marketing Overseas*
*Marketing and the Brand Manager*
*Marketing through Research*
*Marketing and Financial Control*
*Marketing and the Computer*
*Marketing and Work Study*
*Marketing and Economics*
*Marketing: The Use of Advertising*
*Marketing and the Dynamics of Planning*

BERNARD TAYLOR
D. W. SMALLBONE

# EDITOR'S FOREWORD

IN THE study of marketing, sales management tends, along with distribution, to be a Cinderella; and yet within a total of marketing expenditure it is these two which account in many companies for the highest allocation.

There is a dearth of figures, but recent estimates suggest that something like twice the money is spent on sales forces that is spent on advertising.

In view of the large sums of money involved, it could be expected that sales management would have received considerable attention from writers and researchers. Unhappily such does not seem to be the case. Even a superficial survey of recent research, cases written and published literature reveals the scant attention which has been paid to this area of marketing.

The purpose of this book is to explain in simple, easy-to-understand terminology the purpose and structure of a modern sales force and to offer practical suggestions for raising the efficiency of the sales force within the complex of a modern business.

Whilst part of the Essentials of Marketing series could, therefore, be of interest to any serious student of marketing, this volume will also be essential to the *practising* sales manager grappling on a day to day basis with the problems of recruiting, selecting, training, motivating and controlling his sales force.

*Ashridge Management College*              D. W. SMALLBONE

# INTRODUCTION

THIS book is about Systematic Market-orientated Business Management, or "Marketing" for short, and the role of the Sales Manager in a market-orientated business enterprise. This role differs greatly from that of the Sales Manager in a traditional production-orientated business operating in a seller's market.

It is neither a comprehensive reference book about Marketing nor a detailed textbook on the practice of Sales Management. There are already many excellent books dealing with the two subjects in much greater depth. It is, in fact, an outline of the part that Sales Management plays in Marketing as a whole. As such, it fills a real need, because a book on Marketing will include just one chapter on Sales Management out of a total of anything up to thirty chapters. A book on Sales Management, on the other hand, is likely to include just a brief introduction about "The Marketing Concept", followed by, again, anything up to thirty chapters on Sales Management in great detail. This book, therefore, should be useful to the busy sales executive, either to help him consolidate and set in perspective his understanding of his role, and/or as an introduction to more extensive studies in Marketing generally, or Sales Management in particular.

My grateful thanks are due to my colleague Douglas Smallbone for his encouragement and Mrs. Mona Hipwell for her hard work in deciphering my scribble and typing the manuscript.

*Ashridge*                                              F. H. ELSBY

CHAPTER 1

# SYSTEMATIC MARKET-ORIENTATED BUSINESS MANAGEMENT

## INTRODUCTION

BEFORE we look at sales management in particular, let us consider the marketing approach to business management in general. This has been covered in other books in this series, but I repeat it here again, possibly in a slightly different way, so that we are quite clear what it is we are discussing.

Systematic Market-orientated Business Management differs from traditional systems of management in the following ways:

(i)   an open and conscientious attempt is made to recognize problems and opportunities, to assess them objectively and define them clearly;

(ii)  objectives or goals are selected deliberately and, again, defined clearly;

(iii) means consistent with the achievement of the objectives or goals so selected and defined are planned and implemented systematically;

(iv)  in motivating people to achieve results reliance is placed on information, persuasion and clear communication rather than coercive or authoritarian power;

(v)   results are assessed candidly and impartially;

(vi)  data derived from such a review of results provides, *inter alia*, a basis for a review of the objectives or goals and the means selected for their achievement. Better and better standards of approximation are continually sought;

(vii) it is intellectually demanding.

1

This system of management falls into five main areas:

    (i)   Discovery and Research.
   (ii)   Formulation of Policy.
  (iii)   Planning how the policy shall be implemented.
  (iv)   Implementation.
   (v)   Control.

It applies equally to the company as a whole, to departments within the company, and to individuals. If the company as a whole has no clear idea of where it wants to go and how it intends to get there, divisional or departmental policies and plans can neither be made nor implemented; nor can the particular jobs of individuals be specified and their performance appraised.

In several accounts of "Management by Objectives" it has been stated that in the absence of overall corporate policy it is still possible to practice management by objectives at departmental or middle management level. This is nonsense of course. If the objectives of the company have not been declared, the departmental manager cannot establish departmental objectives consistent with those of the company.

For the rest of the chapter we shall be dealing with the application of this system of management at the corporate level. The rest of the book is given to its application in sales management.

## DISCOVERY AND RESEARCH

A company must continually be investigating its external environment and its internal practices and operations. In this system of management it is acknowledged that bright ideas may originate from anywhere—customers, distributors, salesmen, research department, the shop floor, etc. Ideas from top management are submitted to the same objective evaluation that is given to ideas from less prominent sources.

There are four broad areas in which research should be undertaken by a company.

**Into its External Environment:**

*(a) The physical universe—pure and applied technical research*

The pace of technological change is continually accelerating. A company, if it is to survive, must actively pursue a policy of innovation, and continually be developing new technologies, new processes and new products and services.

*(b) The world and national economy—economic research*

Few companies engage in economic research, except the very largest—banks in particular, and university departments of course. Most of us get no further than reading the financial journals.

*(c) The market(s) the company exists to serve; Channels of communication/distribution; Individual customers* ⎫ *market research* ⎬ ⎭

Market research is not particularly new. Sir Thomas Gresham, banker to Queen Elizabeth I in the sixteenth century, was one of the earliest to institute a systematic collection, verification, analysis and interpretation of economic and commercial information as an essential part of his business operations. So did the Rothschilds in a later age. In this century, the manufacturers of fast turnover domestic consumables and their advertising agencies commenced large-scale market investigations in the early twenties.

The necessity for accurate marketing information is still not generally appreciated. The manufacturers of domestic consumable and semi-durable products generally recognize the need more than manufacturers of industrial products.

**Into its Internal Operations:**

*(a) Work study*

Work study in the factory was first attempted by a Derbyshire china manufacturer in the eighteenth century in this country. Frederick Taylor developed the technique in the U.S.A. in the

1890's. Charles Bedaux and Frank and Lillian Gilbreth developed it still further in the early part of this century. Many more refinements have been developed since then.

There are still many companies in this country who have not adopted work study, either on the factory floor, in the office, or the sales force. Factory managers never cease to be amazed at the tremendous increase in efficiency produced by work study allied to an incentive bonus scheme on its first installation.

### (b) Office method study and systems analysis

Again, these techniques are only being accepted slowly by the majority of companies, even when they have already bought a computer.

### (c) Employee attitude surveys

This is rather like Motivation Research, except it is applied to the company's employees rather than its customers. Very few companies indeed have tried this.

### (d) Operational research

This is the name given to a number of advanced scientific techniques of investigation that attempt to solve real-life problems by the construction of models—usually mathematical.

## FORMULATION OF POLICY

Policy-making requires educated judgement of a very high order. This is because however much factual information one might have, numerous assumptions have to be made in formulating a working hypothesis. It helps greatly if these assumptions are right first time, but they rarely are. Unfortunately one of mankind's great failures is being unable to admit error. However, if this obstacle can be overcome it is possible to learn by one's mistakes. Provided that one has sufficient information and considers the assumptions that are being made very carefully, one is not likely to be so disastrously wrong that mistakes cannot be rectified upon review at an early stage.

There are three steps in formulating policy:
- (i) Forecasting;
- (ii) Establishing objectives;
- (iii) Establishing basic operating policies.

## Forecasting

Forecasting involves:
- (a) anticipation of the future effects of past and current events;
- (b) identification of risks and opportunities.

Generally speaking, forecasts should be made for the long, medium and short term ahead into the future.

*Long-term forecasts.* A long-term forecast is essentially speculative in nature and makes no pretence to accuracy. It is an attempt to anticipate the broad changes that are likely to occur in the distant future. In spite of the distortions of abnormal events, wars, famines, *coups d'état,* Acts of God, etc., certain trends have an inevitable momentum; e.g. the growth of the population, increase in life expectancy, technological, economic, social and political change, etc.

Usually a long-term forecast is for a period in excess of 10 years ahead. In making the forecast basic assumptions have to be made and quantitative probabilities ascribed to them. They will never be accurate, but clear definition can provide a point of departure from which the assumptions can be measured as circumstances change and events actually occur. This then provides a basis for modifying or revising the basic assumptions, and thus revising the original forecast.

Long-term objectives based upon such forecasts have to be continually reviewed, usually once a year. This exercise is not a waste of time, since the discipline required to do it tends to orientate one's thoughts towards future opportunities—realistic opportunities, not castles in the air—rather than current problems.

*Medium-term operational forecast.* A medium-term operational forecast is for the period within the range of present executive action. It is the longest period required for the realization of objectives once they have been irrevocably established.

A power-station, for example, takes 5 years to build and commission. The forecast for electric power consumption must therefore be based upon a minimum period of 5 years ahead. Usually such a forecast is for a period of 5 to 10 years ahead.

*Immediate forecast.* The immediate forecast is for the short term, usually the accounting year ahead. It forms the basis for establishing the immediate objectives of the business—sales turnover and profit, the sales targets by products, markets, territories, etc., and for the planning, execution and control of the day-to-day operations necessary to achieve the immediate objectives in terms of human, material and financial resources. The actual budgetary control period is usually less than 1 year. It may be 3 months, 1 month or even a week.

## Establishing Objectives—the future we want to create

Deciding upon the objectives and their priorities of a business enterprise is the key function of management, especially top management. Having considered the environment external to the company and the market(s) in particular, the risks and opportunities, the resources and techniques available, we have to fall back on what is considered "reasonable". Unfortunately there are few reliable yardsticks:

e.g. What is a reasonable profit?
It depends on the risks involved.
How do you measure risks?
That's a matter of judgement. . . .
How do you measure profit?
As a percentage return on capital employed.
How do you measure capital employed?
That's a difficult question to answer. . . .

However, even if initially, the objectives are largely subjective opinions based upon insufficient factual information, they form benchmarks towards which it may be possible to measure progress or the lack of it.

If measurement of progress (or lack of it) is possible, this in turn provides a basis for review and revision of the original objectives.

It is desirable to quantify objectives. Verbal expressions by themselves such as "reasonable", "improved", "increased", "fair", "better", "more", "less", etc., should be avoided wherever possible.

*Examples:*

    (a)  To increase shareholders dividend from 6% to 10%.
    (b)  To increase shareholders dividend from 2/6 to 3/– per share.
    (c)  To increase sales turnover by 30%.
    (d)  To increase sales turnover from £1m. to £1·5m.
    (e)  To increase market share from 12% to 16%.

A business enterprise is a social organism. It is a community of interests. Its principal objective is to survive, which implies change and growth. This can only be achieved if the output of value satisfactions to customers, shareholders, employees, suppliers and society at large is greater than the input of human, financial and material resources (see Fig. 1.1).

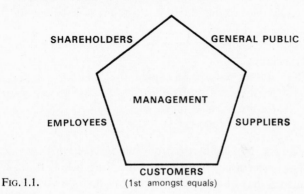

FIG. 1.1.

CUSTOMERS
(1st amongst equals)

The secondary objectives must therefore be framed in terms of the interests of:

(i) *The customers.* This is the heart of the Marketing Concept. Without customers the business cannot possibly survive. The law, as it stands, says that management's prime responsibility is to the shareholders. Some people, on the other hand, believe that the employees' interests come first. However, the interests of neither the shareholders nor the employees can be served, unless the interests of the customers are served first.

Before meaningful objectives can be established, the market(s) the company exists to serve must be specified accurately.

Yardsticks for establishing objectives in terms of customer satisfaction include:

> Volume of sales in units
> Volume of sales in revenue
> Market standing or share
> Quality standards/value for money
> Acceptance of new products

(ii) *The shareholders.* The shareholders are the main risk-takers in the enterprise and as such have to be rewarded commensurately with the particular risks of the business. If it is in show-business, a 1000% return on invested capital may be considered reasonable; if, on the other hand, it is in the distribution of staple food commodities, a net return of less than 10% may be satisfactory.

Yardsticks for establishing objectives in terms of shareholders' satisfaction include:

> Return on original capital invested
> Return on assets employed
> Return on sales turnover
> Growth of assets

(iii) *Employees.* No doubt the trade unions believe that the purpose of a business is simply to provide their members with jobs. Much work has been done by social psychologists on what employees do want. Perhaps it is best not to go too far into this here, except to say that in general they want to earn a reasonable living at a creative and worthwhile job.

Yardsticks for establishing objectives in terms of employee satisfaction include:

> Employee turnover
> Strikes
> Absenteeism
> Productivity

(iv) *Suppliers*. At least suppliers want to be paid and to make a profit out of serving your company. Most companies go no further than just paying on time, but there is great scope for making suppliers more of partners in your own business rather than holding them off at arm's length. In other words, you should help them to help you better.

Yardsticks for establishing objectives in terms of supplier satisfaction include:

> Quality standards
> Credit received
> Speed and frequency of deliveries
> Standards of service generally

(v) *The general public*. Some say "the public be damned". Others carry on to absurd lengths about industry's responsibilities to society at large. Whichever view is taken, there is no doubt that a business enterprise does have certain responsibilities to the public. It should not pollute the air they breathe or the water they drink. Whole towns may be dependent upon the company's prosperity. However large and powerful a company is, it cannot really afford to ignore the interests of the general public.

If a company transgresses the general interest too far, the Government, as agents (not the masters) of the public, can take active measures to prevent any further transgression.

Yardsticks for establishing objectives in terms of satisfaction of the general public include:

Volume of adverse criticism
Legal actions
Official interference

It is true that many companies go no further than a vague generalization about profits as a statement of objectives. However, even if a conscientious attempt is made to formulate a comprehensive statement of corporate objectives, we have two problems.

The first is to quantify the objectives—in some cases this is quite easy, in others impossible. The second is to ascribe meaningful relative weights of importance to each objective. Inevitably they will have to be subjective, but it helps if a numerical scale is used:

| Extremely important | 100 |
| Very important | 75 |
| Important | 50 |
| Not very important | 25 |
| Not important at all | 0 |

The statement of corporate objectives and their relative weights of importance should be drawn up by the top-management team along the following lines:

*Objectives for next year     Importance*

1. To increase sales by 20% from £1m. to £1.2m., and thus achieve a market share of 15%    100
2. To maintain quality at the present standard    80
3. To introduce three new products    50
4. To guarantee a minimum 8% return to shareholders on original investment    100
5. To increase capital assets by 10%    60
6. To reduce employee turnover from 20% to 15%    70
7. To reduce number of days lost by strikes and absenteeism by 25%    30

8. To reduce accidents by 20%    60
9. To increase output of standard hours by 20% without increasing staff    90
10. To persuade and assist supplier X to reduce average delivery times from 12 weeks to 3 weeks    50
11. To conduct the business within the bounds of legality    100
12. To conduct the business in the public interest over and above the requirements of the law    10

This example is a very simple one. In practice the statement of objectives would be quite a lengthy document. It would be a time-consuming job to prepare, since it would require redrafting several times to eliminate inconsistencies in the objectives and their importance ratings. Superficially, this approach appears no more than a matter of common sense, but in fact it is an exercise that demands mental discipline of a very high order.

It is essential that the chairman leading such discussions should be, and be seen to be, completely impartial. There is bound to be much argument. If an exercise like this has never been attempted before, and there is an atmosphere of resentment and mistrust between the executives concerned, then it may be wise to employ an outsider, such as a management consultant, who has absolutely no axe to grind, to lead it.

Whilst it may be a painful experience at the time, this exercise yields tremendous benefits. At one blow, it severs all the "political" knots which cause so much damage to the morale of any organization. The agreement of the executives concerned that the objectives are "reasonable" commits them to their achievement. They have taken the first step in creating the future they want for their company and themselves.

## Establishing Basic Operating Policies

Having decided what we want to do—our objectives—we next have to decide how we shall achieve them—the means. It is essential to distinguish quite clearly between ends and means— all too often they get muddled and much time is wasted discussing the means before the desired ends have been decided or defined.

Information derived from the data-collecting or research stage will suggest several possible courses of action to achieve the same objective. Further analysis is required to determine which of the alternatives is *likely* to prove to be the "best" or optimal course. One can never say categorically that one way *will be* the best, because once having embarked on a particular course of action, circumstances continue to change and one cannot go backwards in time to embark upon a different one to see if it would have been any better.

It helps greatly if the method can be tested experimentally beforehand, either by devising a synthetic model as in operational research, or by conducting a small-scale real-life experiment as in pilot scale manufacturing operations or test marketing.

Still too often one hears the expression "but this is the way we have always done it", or "it may seem odd to you but it works". Just as the objectives require periodic review, so do the methods adopted to achieve them.

## PLANNING

Having decided upon the objectives and the means of achievement in outline, the next stage is to plan the activities—the work to be done—in detail, in four main areas:

> Human Resources
> Material Resources
> Financial Resources
> External Communication

### Human Resources

Most people, by now, are familiar with what an organization chart looks like. It should be borne in mind that an organization chart is a static concept, whereas an organization is a dynamic living thing. By itself the chart tells us very little and it must be qualified by a detailed specification of the objectives of, and means to be adopted by, each division or department, consistent with the objectives and operating policies of the organization as a whole. Also the job to be done by each individual must be specified:

> The objectives of the job.
> Quantitative targets.
> His powers—the limits of his authority and responsibility, making sure that they are consistent.

His relationships with other departments and individuals within the organization and with outside organizations and individuals.

His duties:

His title on the organization chart, by itself, is insufficient.

Having defined the job the individual is to perform, it is then possible to decide the right kind of man, his qualifications and personal qualities, to do the job. If the job to be done is not specified, the right man for the job cannot be specified. Furthermore, with a clear job specification it becomes possible to judge, later on, how well the man is doing the job and whether he needs further training.

## Material Resources

The requirements in terms of physical material resources, consistent with achieving the objectives, also have to be planned and specified:

> Property
> Plant
> Machinery
> Raw materials
> Work in progress
> Finished goods

The essence of the marketing concept is that production is planned to meet a known or anticipated customer demand, rather than to make what we know we can make and then try to sell it. Nevertheless, it is not unknown for firms to have made substantial investment in new factories only to discover that no one wanted the output. This is excusable in the case of radically new products where market research and forecasting likely demand is extremely difficult, if not impossible; but the really expensive mistakes have usually been made in well-established markets with well-established products where new facilities have been built for non-economic reasons, such as prestige.

## Financial Resources

*Pricing.* Pricing policy as one of the principal means of achieving the objectives of the business must be consistent with them. It must also be consistent with the other means employed in achieving the objectives. The selling price of the product/service properly set, provides the funds to pay for all the other activities within the business consistent with the attainment of its objectives.

Pricing is a matter of judgement. There are no neat formulae for calculating what the "right" price ought to be. In the absence of clearly defined objectives this decision can be no more than an intuitive guess. There are five general objectives in pricing, which have to be considered altogether and a compromise agreed as to their relative importance:

> to achieve a given target of profitability;
> to support a planned market position;
> to pre-empt, meet or follow competition;
> to differentiate product or company image;
> to achieve stabilisation of price.

Provided the objectives are clearly defined, the tools of economic, market and cost analysis can serve as valuable aids to judgement in making the decision.

*The budget.* A budget is a financial statement of the company's objectives and the means of their achievement. That is, the sales/ revenue and profit objectives and the necessary costs incurred by each department or cost centre of the company in the achievement of its own particular objectives, consistent with the overall objectives of the enterprise.

## External Communication

The business communicates with the outside world in a number of ways.

The principal means of communication is the product the company is making and/or the service it provides. The product/ service must be carefully specified, both in the producer's or seller's own terms *and* in terms of the values—the benefits and advantages—to the buyer.

Having specified exactly what it is we are selling, we are then in a position to plan our sales messages—in language appropriate to the target audience, and how we are going to deliver them. We may choose to use a sales force, or media advertising, or point of sale promotion, or public relations, either by themselves or in any combination.

We also have to plan how we are going to deliver the product/ service to its eventual user. Again we usually have a considerable range of choice in the means of delivery.

## IMPLEMENTATION

Having done our research; decided upon our objectives; decided upon our basic operating policies; planned the work to be done in detail; we are now in a position to implement the plan. Again implementation is in four main areas.

### People

Implementation of the plan in terms of the people required to carry out the work involves:

> Recruiting
> Selecting
> Training
> Direction
> Motivation

None of these activities can be done successfully in the absence of a clear job specification or description. Translating the job specification into the specification of the man to do the job is a matter of judgement and there are no facile formulae, such as X school, Y university and Z regiment. Every job is different and every individual is different. Fitting the right man to the right job is a vitally important and exceedingly difficult management task. It is to be hoped that, by now, notions of having standard men for standard jobs—the administrator's dream—have been dispelled.

Having decided upon the profile of qualifications and personal qualities of the man required to do the job, we are now in a position to start recruiting, either by publicly advertising the job, by personal solicitation, or by a variety of other means. If public advertising is used, the advert should include a brief statement of the job specification, the man profile and the terms offered. Thus the advertisement itself will start the selection procedure. People are usually fairly honest with themselves and will tend to apply only for those jobs which they think they would like and for which they are suited. Inevitably some cranks will apply. If the advert is a vaguely worded one about "opportunities unlimited" you will either get hundreds of replies or none at all.

Selection of the right man may then be further narrowed down by the use of application forms and interviews. The purpose of an interview is to establish the facts about the candidate and to find out whether there is a coherent pattern in his behaviour. Evaluation of the suitability of the candidate for the job should be done after, not during, the interview. Even the most expertly conducted interview can never be entirely reliable and it is best to have at least two, conducted by different people. If the interviewer does not have a clear idea of the job to be done and the kind of man he is looking for, the interview will be a complete waste of time and a wholly unreliable method of selection.

Having selected the man, who will never conform to the ideal we are looking for, we are then in a position to decide what training he needs. Most people these days will agree that training is a "jolly good thing"—it is the "in" thing to have. However, in the absence of a job specification and the ideal man profile for the job, we can form no judgement about the individual's strengths and weaknesses, and thus what purpose the training is to achieve. In these circumstances, any training will do.

Direction and delegation are achieved by means of the job specification. You cannot direct a man to do a job if you yourself do not have a clear idea of what it is you want him to do. Neither can you delegate responsibility and the requisite authority.

Again, if you have no clear idea of the job to be performed you cannot motivate a man to do it. No amount of shouting, threats, perks or bribes will be of any avail.

Most people like to work within clear terms of reference, so the job specification itself is part of the process of motivation. In addition, it is essential that the individual should agree that the job is within his capabilities and the reward is reasonable. Commitment to a clearly defined objective is one of the most powerful motivating froces known.

Further motivation is provided by:

giving him all the information he needs to do the job;

training—building his strengths and minimising the effects of his weaknesses;

informing him how he is progressing towards his objectives.

If all these conditions are satisfied, ordinary people can achieve extraordinary results, and, what is more, enjoy doing it.

Only now, at this stage, can we actually get on with running:

Manufacturing operations—actually making the goods.

Financial operations,

cash flows,

borrowing,

investment.

Selling operations,

the sales force,

advertising,

sales promotion,

public relations,

distribution.

### CONTROL

The final stage in this system of management is Control. In traditional systems of management, the word control is taken to mean restriction or even coercion, and it appears to the subjects of it, to be exercised arbitrarily or wilfully.

In this system of management the process of control is quite specifically that:

> objectives, goals, targets or standards are established;
> the variance between the actual performance achieved and that desired is measured objectively;
> action is taken to ensure that future performance conforms to the desired standard.

This process should be continuous and carried out in every sphere of activity of the company. The chief instrument of control is the budget.


## Budgetary Control

Traditional or "historical" accounting systems show (usually in the most general terms) what has happened in the most recent period compared with what happened the time before. The "time before" is the only comparison, or standard of performance. Clearly such "historical" systems can provide no control at all, since control can only be exercised if what is actually happening can be compared with what should be happening according to plan.

Budgetary control is the measurement of the activities within the enterprise reduced to monetary terms so that management can see which activities need adjusting to bring them into conformity with the overall objectives of the enterprise. Control is only effected when the necessary adjustments in activities have been made.

Deviations from the planned course are reported as variances. Since the budget is prepared as an estimate of costs based on an estimate of sales, some tolerance is required, say $\pm 5\%$. Provided the variance is within these limits, management can be by exception; concentrating only on those activities whose performance lies outside these limits—either way, positive or negative (see Table 1.1).

TABLE 1.1

Example: Budget for XYZ Co. Ltd. for next year

| Sales Income | | | £300,000 |
|---|---|---|---|
| **Expenses** | *Fixed* (£) | *Variable* (£) | *Total* (£) |
| Direct materials | | 117,000 | 117,000 |
| Direct labour | 32,000 | 16,000 | 48,000 |
| Production | | | |
| Indirect labour (inc. chargehands) | 7600 | 2000 | 9600 |
| Management salaries (inc. foreman) | 3500 | | 3500 |
| Consumable stores | | 2750 | 2750 |
| Depreciation, plant and machinery | 1000 | | 1000 |
| Power | 200 | 1000 | 1200 |
| Works Manager's bonus | | 250 | 250 |
| Building repairs | 500 | | 500 |
| Machinery maintenance | 400 | | 400 |
| Totals | 13,200 | 6000 | 19,200 |
| Selling | | | |
| Sales Manager's salary | 2500 | | 2500 |
| Salesmen's salaries | 15,000 | | 15,000 |
| Commissions | | 9500 | 9500 |
| Travelling, cars, etc. | 7500 | | 7500 |
| Discounts | | 5900 | 5900 |
| Advertising, sales promotion | 15,000 | | 15,000 |
| Totals | 40,000 | 15,400 | 55,400 |
| Administration and Distribution | | | |
| General Manager's salary | 3000 | | 3000 |
| Office salaries | 5600 | | 5600 |
| Office light and heat | 200 | | 200 |
| Telephones | 40 | 85 | 125 |
| Office general expenses | 2150 | | 2150 |
| Packer's wages | 500 | | 500 |
| Packing materials | | 1650 | 1650 |
| Driver's wages | 2000 | | 2000 |
| Vans—running expenses | | 3000 | 3000 |
| Vans—depreciation | 2000 | | 2000 |
| Insurance | 2050 | 2000 | 4050 |
| Totals | 17,540 | 6735 | 24,275 |
| Grand Totals | 102,740 | 161,135 | 263,875 |
| Profit before Tax | | | 36,125 |

Expenses have been classified into either fixed or variable. Variable expenses vary directly with sales/production. Fixed expenses do not vary significantly between say, 60% to 100% of the company's sales/production.

An operating budget would, of course, be broken down into much greater detail for each department or cost centre. This simple example is to illustrate the principle.

The budgetary control report for, say, the 1st quarter of the new year, could be as shown in Table 1.2.

The budget can be summarized in the form of a break-even chart as shown in Fig. 1.2.

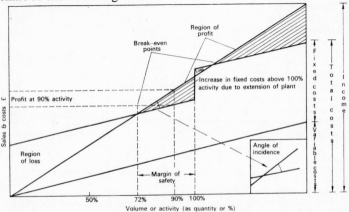

FIG. 1.2. A Break-even Chart

The following conclusions can be drawn from a break-even chart:

1. The break-even point is advanced by an increase in:
   (a) fixed costs, which usually have a greater influence,
   (b) variable costs,
   or a decrease in revenue.
2. The magnitude of the angle of incidence is determined by the ratio of variable costs to sales. It is not influenced by the fixed costs. It is necessary therefore to control the variable costs in order to maintain the rate at which profit expands.

Examples of the relationship between the break-even point and the angle of incidence:

1.  Low break-even point, large angle of incidence. Typical of low variable cost business with small fixed costs, e.g. an advertising agency.
2.  High break-even point, large angle of incidence. Typical of highly capitalized industry, which is fairly profitable, e.g. heavy engineering.
3.  High break-even point, small angle of incidence. Typical of a highly capitalized industry with a poor profit, e.g. British Rail.
4.  Low break-even point, small angle of incidence. Typical of an industry with low fixed costs and not a very high profit, e.g. many poorly managed small firms.

## Some Common Complaints about Budgetary Control

1. "It does not work." This is usually said by people when a budgetary control system has only been working for a year or two. It can take up to 5 years to get a system operating properly. The following factors are prerequisite:

(a)  The objectives of the enterprise are clearly defined.

(b)  The means are clearly defined and accurately costed. The knowledge gained by detailed investigation into the causes of variances from budget will enable more accurate sales targets and cost estimates to be made in future budgets.

2. "The sales targets are always too high." It is agreed that sales forecasts can never be perfectly accurate. However, when sales are consistently below the target, it is often too readily assumed that the target is unrealistic.

Whilst the target ought certainly to be kept under continuous review, it should not be revised without thorough market investigation, just to conform to the actual sales performance. This completely vitiates the whole purpose of having a budgetary control system. Superficially the system might appear to be work-

TABLE 1.2

| | Budget | Actual | Variance + more than Budget Tolerance ±5% | | Variance − less than Budget Tolerance ±5% | | Action | Remarks |
|---|---|---|---|---|---|---|---|---|
| | £ | £ | £ | % | £ | % | | |
| Sales income | 75,000 | 78,000 | 3000 | 4 | | | | |
| Direct materials | 29,300 | 35,000 | 5700 | 19 | | | * | Wastage due to lower-grade labour |
| Direct labour | 12,000 | 11,000 | | | 1000 | 8 | * | Lower-grade Labour employed |
| Production | | | | | | | | |
| Indirect labour (inc. chargehands) | 2400 | 1500 | | | 900 | 38 | * | Two left, not replaced |
| Management salaries (inc. foreman) | 875 | 875 | | | | | | |
| Consumable stores | 690 | 750 | 60 | 9 | | | * | Wastage by lower-grade labour |
| Depreciation, plant & machinery | 250 | 250 | | | | | | |
| Power | 300 | 400 | 100 | 25 | | | * | Wastage by lower-grade labour |

| | Budget | Actual | Over £ | Over % | Under £ | Under % | * | * | |
|---|---|---|---|---|---|---|---|---|---|
| Works Manager's bonus | 62 | | | | 62 | 100 | | * | Forfeited |
| Building repairs | 125 | | | | 125 | 100 | | * | Not done |
| Machinery maintenance | 100 | 100 | | | | | | | |
| **Selling** | | | | | | | | | |
| Sales Manager's salary | 625 | 625 | | | | | | | |
| Salesmen's salaries | 3750 | 3750 | | | | | | | |
| Commissions | 2380 | 2500 | 120 | 5 | | | | | |
| Travelling, cars, etc. | 1880 | 1940 | 60 | 3 | | | | | |
| Discounts | 1475 | 1350 | | | 125 | 8 | | * | Quantities on individual orders not large enough to qualify |
| Advertising, sales promotion | 3750 | 3850 | 100 | 3 | | | | | |
| **Administration and Distribution** | | | | | | | | | |
| General Manager's salary | 750 | 750 | | | | | | | |
| Office salaries | 1400 | 1300 | | | 100 | 7 | | * | One typist left, not replaced |
| Office light and heat | 50 | 60 | 10 | 20 | | | * | | Cold spell |
| Telephones | 31 | 30 | | | 1 | 3 | | | |
| Office general expenses | 537 | 540 | 3 | 1 | | | | | |
| Packer's wages | 125 | 135 | 10 | 8 | | | * | | Excess overtime |
| Packing materials | 412 | 500 | 88 | 21 | | | * | | Repacking of returned goods |
| Driver's wages | 500 | 550 | 50 | 10 | | | * | | Excess overtime |
| Vans—running expenses | 750 | 785 | 35 | 5 | | | | | |
| Vans—depreciation | 500 | 500 | | | | | | | |
| Insurance | 1012 | 1012 | | | | | | | |

* costs which are above or below budget, i.e. where action is required.

ing perfectly, but in fact it will amount to little more than "going through the motions"—no real control will exist.

3. "The budget is sacrosanct and inflexible. It stifles managerial initiative, etc."

This sort of complaint arises when the budget is seen as an end in itself and not as the means to an end.

Things that quite obviously need to be done, such as an extra expenditure for a special sales promotion, new machinery, a deserved pay rise, etc., are denied because they are not in the budget.

No budget is ever perfect, simply because the future cannot be foreseen with perfect accuracy. Budgets must be flexible and provision made for the unforeseen. If it is agreed that a particular unforeseen operation and its associated expense is necessary, then it should be carried out.

This attitude also leads to the juggling of figures. If the budgeted sales have been reached before the end of the period, invoices are held over until the next period. Similarly for all the other items of the budget, production, raw materials, deviations of all kinds are juggled so that they appear to conform to the budget.

4. "Too much paper work!" Certainly the introduction of a budgetary control system will call for more and better records, but this is not necessarily a bad thing.

Paper work will become excessive when managers demand to see *all* the figures. This is impractical and unnecessary. The purpose of the control system is to draw attention to the deviations from the budget so that action can be taken to adjust performance into conformity with the planned course of activity, i.e. management by exception.

In the initial stages, there will be numerous deviations. As time goes by, and the causes of these deviations are discovered and corrected, the number of deviations reported at any one time will tend to decrease and so will the amount of paper involved.

A computer can produce an astronomical amount of information if *all* the figures are required. On the other hand, it can also digest and condense all of it into as little as one page of "action" information.

5. Variances which show a saving in expenditure are considered "good" and no further attention is paid to them.

Variances showing either a saving or an excess of expenditure outside the tolerance limits of the budget are both "bad".

## AN ILLUSTRATIVE CASE HISTORY
### Contractor's Plant & Engineering Co. Ltd.
#### *Background Information*

The company was formed in the late 1880's as a family concern, and is located in a small east coast town. The factory buildings were originally located on the outskirts of the town, but were later completely surrounded by residential properties which prevent enlargement of the premises. Material storage accommodation for structural steels and an erection yard about one mile distant from the factory were secured in 1946.

During the 1930's the company was acquired as a subsidiary of a large civil engineering undertaking. Since then the company has grown considerably. Over the last 30 years output has grown from £350,000 to £1,850,000, of which £410,000 is exports. During the late 1950's there were several changes in the management structure and in the personnel. Several isolated attempts were made to modify the plant layout and to improve the planning and control aspects of production; none of these were outstandingly successful.

The company is engaged in medium to heavy engineering and manufactures mainly to customers' requirements, but from time to time accepts orders to manufacture long runs of repetitive work to customers' drawing and specifications. The non-repetitive work varies considerably and includes special-purpose cranes, excavators, scrapers, conveyors and haulage plant. The repetitive work has included such items as heavy-duty conveyor drums, jacks for the aircraft industry and pumps of various sizes and types.

Sales are made mainly by direct contact with the user and all salesmen are technically qualified engineers.

Overall production cycle times range from a few days for spares, which frequently have to be dealt with expeditiously, to 18 months or more for major items. Design and production of many jobs proceed concurrently.

The Managing Director has complained that there is an increasing tendency to lose customers' goodwill by failing to meet delivery promises and that this also leads to excessive erection costs. Broken delivery promises seem to result from two main causes. The first is that the work load on the factory floor, although reasonably balanced from month to month in total figures, calls for fluctuating demands on certain sections of the works, thus creating restrictions and subsequent delays. The second cause seems to stem from lack of liaison between the works and design department with the result that drawings come to the works in the wrong order, many being too late for fitting into the planned schedule of work. The Managing Director claims that profits are reasonable and have not so far been deteriorating appreciably. He is a little disturbed at the future prospects, however, should the order book be affected by bad customer relations arising from inferior service.

## Personnel and General Organization

### *General*

The Managing Director is the only director with executive duties. He has no connection with the original owners but has been with the company since he was 14 years old. He is an extremely hard-working man who, although a fully qualified mechanical engineer, has spent most of his life on the sales side; it is estimated that he is in his late 50's. The personnel answering to him number 767 and they are organized into six distinct groups.

## Estimating and Sales

The personnel consists of a Sales Manager who is 42 years of age and who answers directly to the Managing Director. His sales staff numbers seven, two of whom deal exclusively with the parent company. There is a secretarial and clerical staff of ten. Each sales engineer compiles his own estimates in collaboration with the Chief Designer and Managing Director. The sales staff control the overall works load on the factory and forecast delivery promises by allocating the wage content of orders received to the appropriate months ahead.

Estimates are frequently based on previous order costs but sometimes, where there is little to go on, a general arrangement drawing and a bill of quantities is produced in the Drawing Office.

## Buying

The Buyer, who is non-technical, has been 42 years with the Company and is now 57 years old. He answers directly to the Managing Director and has one assistant and a secretarial staff of four. Most instructions stem directly from the Drawing Office in the form of material requisitions, and items that are "technically difficult" are bought either by the Chief Designer or by the sales engineers.

## Design

The Chief Designer is 58 years of age and answers directly to the Managing Director. His staff, which numbers forty-one, is split into two sections, each controlled by an Assistant Designer and a few section leaders; both Assistant Designers are in their 60's. Broadly, the intention is for one Assistant Designer to supervise work concerned with the mechanical engineering industry and for the other to concentrate on general engineering. In practice both assistants supervise work in the other's field so as to keep the work load equitable. Draughtsmen are seldom transferred from one section to the other unless the arrangement is permanent or the draughtsman is being trained. Much of the work is concerned with the adaptation of existing designs but there is a substantial amount of original design.

## Production

Works management, works engineering, site erection and production planning and control, including stores, are all the responsibility of the Works Manager who answers directly to the Managing Director. He appears to be a very capable person but suffers from ill health. Answering to him as Deputy Works Manager is a recently appointed engineer of 38 whose duties are difficult to determine. This man seems to have had little education or formal technical training but seems to handle labour extremely well and to have spent much of his time on plant erection. The total works personnel amounts to 668.

The works comprise the usual departments found in a general engineering factory. The production planning and control department (exclusive of the stores personnel) consists of twelve people under the control of a middle-aged, active and intelligent ex-foreman. The outside erection staff consists of eight experienced riggers who are supplemented from time to time by selected works personnel but normally they hire local assistance for erection jobs.

The stores set-up seems rather peculiar and comprises:

*General Stores*—storekeeper, plus five men who answer to the Works Manager.

*Bar Store*—two men who answer to the Machine Shop foreman.

*Steel Sections and Plate Store*—this is an open storage area in the main factory area and it is manned by one labourer and one craneman under the control of the Material Preparation Squad foreman. This squad operates saws, guillotines, punches and plate-burning machines and equipment.

*Erection Yard Store* (remote from factory area)—two men part-time storekeeping and part-time labouring who answer to Erection Shop foreman.

*Pattern Shop Stores*—controlled when necessary by a labourer
and the foreman.

*Foundry Stores*—controlled when necessary by the foreman.

## Secretarial and Accounting

The Company Secretary, who is 56, answers directly to the
Managing Director and with a staff of two also acts as official
cashier. He controls all accounting and wage computation
procedures through a Chief Clerk who has a staff of twenty-four
and has a considerable knowledge of accounting techniques,
although not a qualified accountant. Historical job costing is
practised plus a monthly control on overhead expenditure which
is expressed as a percentage of labour costs.

## Despatch

Much of the company's production goes overseas and because
of this the Clerk answers directly to the Managing Director.
He has one assistant and a secretarial staff of two, but most
financial documents and sometimes shipping documents are
handled jointly by him and the Chief Clerk. Occasionally the
more complicated financial matters are handled by the Managing
Director.

## Products

Orders for heavy mechanical handling plant tend to be placed
cyclically, the larger orders for the U.K. usually reaching the
company within two to three months of the National Budget
date. Orders for general engineering equipment and spares flow
in at a fairly steady level. Sub-contract work from the parent
company amounting to about 25% of the total fluctuates considerably in volume from month to month.

The company holds an excellent reputation in the mechanical
handling field and sells largely on its reputation for quality and
reliability for service. Delivery on schedule is frequently the

essence of the contract and in recent years the company has been tending to fall down on delivery promises. Probably half the company's output, including spares, comes into this category and in general, profit margins on mechanical handling appliances and particularly on spares are substantially higher than is the case with other products.

Spares can seldom be held in stock because so much of the production is custom built. In some cases castings and forgings can be held in the part-machined state.

### Materials

The value of the materials amounts to about one-third of the total cost of production. Fairly large stocks of structural steel sections and bars are held and it is on the basis of holding these stocks that the company is able to quote competitive delivery dates. From time to time the Drawing Office calls up special sections involving considerable delay in the procurement of materials and this can account for late delivery. Considerable difficulty is experienced in trying to get the Drawing Office either to work to the stocks held or to specify stocks which should be held. Stockholding is mainly at the discretion of the Buyer but occasionally he puts items in stock at the request of responsible members of the Drawing Office and sales staffs.

Material requisitions are prepared by operatives from drawing lists, as and when required. The slips are initialled by foremen and presented to the stores by operatives or labourers. Ultimately the materials are costed from the requisitions.

### Labour

Labour cost accounts for approximately a quarter of the total cost of production. Incentive schemes are in operation, but they are largely related to bargained standards. The bonus element is low in relation to the fixed wages and by and large the incentives may be classed as ineffective. A considerable amount of overtime working occurs and a small amount of shift working from time to time. There is not much alternative employment in the district and wages are rather depressed when compared with national levels.

The labour is highly skilled and flexible in its use, e.g. turners will readily operate "unskilled" machines without creating awkward precedents. In many cases fitters can work as turners and vice versa.

## *Production Planning and Control Procedure*

When drawings are issued by the Drawing Office one copy goes to production control. Two copies go to a drawing store for shop use and one copy goes to the Pattern Shop when castings are involved. Each drawing may illustrate from one to thirty components, usually associated with the same assembly but with little attempt to separate like materials or components.

Each drawing is examined as soon as it is received in the Production Control Department and is marked with a starting and finishing date. This assessment is made without reference to a production plan and is based on experience and the delivery date. The delivery date is obtained from a copy of the works order prepared in the Sales Department. At this stage instructions are compiled and issued for the production of jigs, fixtures, templates and special tools. The drawing is then filed according to the starting date.

The operative clocks on and off on the job ticket and on completion of each operation the batch and the job ticket pass to an inspection table. The drawing is drawn from the drawing store and returned by the operative.

The inspector draws drawings from the store as required and on completion of inspection stamps the operative's card and items of importance. He then instructs a labourer where the parts should go for the next operation.

On completion all finished parts are sent to a dump in the appropriate assembly or erection department.

Most assembly work is not on bonus and the fitters use time sheets. Sometimes assembly and erection is on a piecework basis and in this case also the men use time-sheets.

Progress chasing is done by men who are each responsible for several contracts or spares or a particular client, e.g. the parent company. The procedure varies considerably and ranges from the preparation of lists of important parts from the drawings, to scrutinizing the job cards in the Machine Shop time office (the cards being laid out by date and by machine type), to chasing to urge lists supplied by the customers.

Copies of orders for all materials (without prices) are passed to the Production Control Department. A clerk is responsible for urging this material and seems to work partly on experience and partly on urge lists prepared by progress chasers. In cases of special difficulty the matter is referred to the Buyer for urging. Steel sections and plates are mainly ordered direct from the mills for stock and such orders are urged by the Buyer.

No attempt is made to assess the load on the various departments as it is known that the overall load is about right. "Bottlenecks" occur at various production points intermittently and this is not helped when progress chasers bring considerable pressure on foremen and machine set-ups have to be disturbed for urgent work. In fairness it must be stated that this mainly applies to spares carrying a high degree of priority. Spares service is considered to be very important by all levels of management, but it appears to produce "hidden" costs.

### Comment

The company's products have not changed appreciably over the years so that production methods are fairly well established and the foremen are usually familiar with the components and their sequence of assembly. Collaboration between foremen is good and there is a high degree of loyalty to the company. Most of the foremen have long service records, however, and it is believed that resistance to change would be very strong.

**Conclusions and Recommendations**

The following conclusions can be drawn from this case history:

The history of delivery failures in Contractor's Plant & Engineering Co. Ltd. is only a symptom of deeper and more serious weaknesses in the management of the company.

Essentially the company is engaged in four markets:

    (a)  mechanical handling;

    (b)  mechanical handling spares;

    (c)  repetitive engineering;

    (d)  jobbing engineering.

At present time there is a complete lack of marketing information in all these areas.

No attempt has been made to investigate or to develop new product ideas suitable for the mechanical handling market.

Little or no attempt has been made to study and improve production methods. There are no objective work standards.

There are no accurate cost data.

As a result, therefore, the company lacks any coherent policy. In the absence of marketing data, forecasting is impossible. Neither corporate nor departmental objectives and operating policies have been established.

No attempt has been made, in the absence of a corporate policy, to plan the activities to be done in order to achieve any objectives.

There is no organization plan. The jobs that the individuals are expected to perform are not specified. Since many of the company's employees are well into middle age, it is apparent that no thought has been given to succession.

There is neither a plan for the utilization of material resources, nor financial resources, nor in terms of how the company intends to communicate with its market.

In the absence of any forward planning it is not surprising that there is an increasing tendency to lose customer's goodwill by failing to meet delivery promises.

Finally, such a situation is impossible to control.

Recommendations, in outline, for improving the situation would be along the following lines.

*In the short term:*

(i) A continuous programme of market research should be started. This should show:

the size of each market;
own and competitor's shares;
market trends.

(ii) A continuous programme of work study should be initiated to provide standard time and cost data, to improve operating methods and to enable the utilization of labour and productive resources to be planned and controlled. At a later stage a labour incentive payment scheme could be introduced.

(iii) On the basis of market research data, forecasts should be made and sales and profit objectives set for each product or product group. These should be:

| | |
|---|---|
| short term | monthly for the next quarter; |
| medium term | quarterly for the next year, to be reviewed quarterly; |
| long term | yearly for the next 5 years, to be reviewed annually. |

(iv) On the basis of sales forecasts and accurate cost and time data, the production planning and control section should plan the loading of the works and only they should give delivery promises.

(v) The sales forecasts should also be used to prepare quarterly departmental budgets which would then be used as the basis for budgetary control.

(vi) Individual product profitabilities should be determined and those that make no contribution to overheads and profit should be eliminated. Sales effort should be concentrated on the products yielding the greatest contribution.

(vii) In order to enable the salesmen to devote their time to prospecting for profitable business, a separate estimating department should be set up. The requirements of the parent company will be attended to by this new department, and not by the salesmen.

(viii) The Managing Director and Sales Manager should go on a suitable course of management development with the emphasis on Marketing.

*In the long term:*

(a) *Marketing.* In conjunction with the design department, new products should be developed to anticipate market trends and customer needs.

(b) *Finance.* More detailed financial objectives should be prepared. A standard costing and budgetary control system should be developed based upon better forecasting procedures and accurate labour and material standards.

(c) *Production.* A value analysis team should be set up to appraise each product and/or part and set material standards. More sophisticated production planning and control procedures should be developed. Stock control procedures should be linked to the sales forecasts to ensure that minimum capital is tied up in stocks.

(d) *Personnel.* A personnel manager should be appointed to advise on personnel policy. A suitable organization structure should be devised, in keeping with the developing forward policies of the company. Job specifications should be drawn up for, and agreed with, each individual. A programme of management training and succession should be initiated.

(e) *Premises.* Consideration should be given to selling the main site and moving to the outskirts of the town.

# CHAPTER 2

# THE SALES MANAGER'S JOB

THE Sales Manager's job will differ greatly from company to company. In the large company his job might only be to direct, motivate and control the activities of the sales force in the field. All other activities would be carried out by the Brand or Product Managers, Personnel Managers, Training Managers, Sales Promotion Executives, etc. In the medium-sized company or smaller enterprise he may be wearing several executive hats and be responsible for much broader aspects of sales and marketing generally.

It may be as well, therefore, if we list all the responsibilities that a Sales Manager could have. He may have to carry out all these functions himself; or he may delegate responsibility to others for carrying out certain functions; or he may have responsibility delegated to him for only some of them. The job specification would have to be decided according to the circumstances in each individual case.

The code letters—(S) for Sales Manager, (M) for Marketing Manager—are used to indicate what are generally agreed to be the respective areas of responsibility. Where there is no general agreement they are bracketed together (S or M).

## 1. Discovery and Research

   (a) Evaluation of new product ideas (M).
   (b) Commissioning market research (S or M).
   (c) Commissioning work study into the activities of the sales force (S).

(d)  Commissioning operational research studies into the warehousing and distribution system (S or M).

(e)  Commissioning employee-attitude surveys (S).

## 2. Formulation of Policy

(a)  Sales forecasting (S or M).

(b)  Establishing sales objectives (S or M) in terms of:
>                 market standing,
>                 quantities,
>                 revenue,
>                 profitability,

by products/services, territories, customer classification.

(c)  Establishing basic operating policies—Marketing/Sales Strategy (S or M).

The appropriate mix of media for communicating with the market:

| | |
|---|---|
| The product/service itself | (M) |
| Pricing | (S or M) |
| Sales Force | (S) |
| Advertising | (M) |
| Sales Promotion | (M) |
| Public Relations | (M) |
| Warehousing and Distribution | (S or M) |

## 3. Planning the Operations of the Sales Force (S)

>         Organization structure
>         Territories
>         Job specifications and man profiles

## 4. Implementation (S)

>         Recruiting
>         Selecting
>         Training
>         Direction
>         Motivation

## 5. Control of the Sales Force Operations (S)

> Evaluation of performance
> Review of objectives and strategy

## 6. Warehousing and Distribution Management (S or M)

All those responsibilities that *could* be part of the sales Manager's job will be considered in the succeeding chapters of this book —bearing in mind that not every Sales Manager will be responsible for all aspects of the total job.

Many of these topics are also considered in greater depth in other books in this series. Further reference should be made to the following:

*Marketing Overseas*
*Marketing and the Brand Manager*
*Marketing through Research*
*Marketing and Financial Control*
*Marketing and the Computer*
*Marketing and Work Study*

# CHAPTER 3

# DISCOVERY AND RESEARCH

### THE ORIGIN OF BRIGHT IDEAS

THE process of discovery is not one which is clearly understood. Necessity may be the mother of invention, but that is not to say that invention is an orphan. Luck and intuition play a part in its genesis, and objective evaluation or research may be said to be the midwife.

The workings of the human mind have been the subject of much study, and these studies have been fruitful. The electronic computer is the nearest we have reached in the creation of artificial intelligence. But the computer requires detailed instructions, complete and accurate information in order to function. The human mind, on the other hand, appears to be able to make accurate guesses even when the data is inadequate in quality and quantity. This mysterious process we call intuition. Some people will deny its existence or its value, and indeed its adjective "intuitive" is sometimes used to mean "ill-informed" or "irrational", but since omniscience is forever denied us we have ultimately to rely on intuition or judgement. The more information we have and the better its quality, the more likely we are to reach the right conclusions.

That luck plays a part in discovery cannot be denied either. Bright ideas can originate anywhere, and even from the most unlikely sources. The ability to perceive relationships which no one else has noticed is apparently not the privilege of a select group of genii.

It is important to recognize this in business management. Bright ideas can come from anywhere; top, middle and supervising levels of management, the research people, salesmen, customers, distributors and the shop floor. It is not unknown for an idea originating from the obscurest of sources to have revolutionized an industry. Some humble person may have had a "bee in his bonnet" clamouring to be let out for years. On careful assessment it may prove to be worthless, but it may well prove to be an insight of genius.

Whatever the source then, bright ideas should be subjected to careful objective evaluation or research. The kinds of research that the sales manager may be concerned with are:

Market Research.

Work Study in the operations of the Sales Force.

Operational Research studies into the company's warehousing and distribution systems.

Employee-attitude Surveys.

He will almost certainly not be required to conduct these studies; he may be required to commission them; he will *most certainly* be concerned with the findings and conclusions from such investigations.

### MARKET RESEARCH

Market research is the term given to the process of finding out in detail:

What can be sold?
To whom?
In what quantities?
At what price?
How?
Where?
When?

It is essential that as much of this information as possible is known in order to plan objectives and their means of achievement on the basis of fact rather than relying entirely on guesswork.

The purpose of market research is the same in both consumer and industrial markets, either at home or overseas. The questions are the same; the answers will be unique to each individual case and the techniques of investigation will be different.

## What Can be Sold?

The products/services that the company is making or providing must be specified very carefully, both in the seller's own terms—technical specification, design, materials, standard costs and times, supporting services, etc.; *and* in terms of the values to the ultimate user and any intermediary involved—the benefits in general and the advantages over direct and indirect competitors in particular.

The sales manager will rarely be deeply involved with product/service policies:

development of new products;

modifications to established products;

product range rationalization.

He will, however, require *all* the relevant information in order to formulate his sales policies and plan, implement and control sales operations.

## To Whom?

The sales manager is most certainly concerned deeply and intimately with the company's customers—the ultimate users of the product/service *and* intermediaries such as distributors, assemblers or converters.

Markets are generally classified as Consumer or Industrial, as shown in Table 3.1.

## In What Quantities and at What Price?

The sales manager will certainly be concerned with establishing sales targets by product group, sales territories and customer classification. He may or may not be intimately concerned with pricing policies. Nevertheless the two are very closely related since demand, and thus quantity that will be sold, is a function of the price.

We shall be considering forecasting and the establishment of sales targets in Chapter 4 and pricing in Chapter 9. Market research data is essential to both.

TABLE 3.1

| Consumer markets | Industrial markets |
|---|---|
| Private individuals behaving in a variety of different roles:<br>  (i) Men: as breadwinners, fathers, husbands, taxpayers, motorists, householders, etc.<br> (ii) Women: as housekeepers, mothers, wives, lovers, hostesses, etc.<br>(iii) Adolescents: as college or school boys and girls, students, "Yobs, Hippies, Mods or Rockers," etc.<br>(iv) Children: as school boys, toddlers, babies, etc.<br>Everybody in fact. Whilst this may be obvious, it is important to realize that individuals will behave quite differently according to the role they are playing at the time. Thus a woman will be a fairly shrewd buyer as the family housekeeper, but irrational when buying clothes or cosmetics |   (i) All kinds of commercial and industrial enterprise, including the nationalized industries:<br>    e.g. Aircraft manufacturers<br>        Banks<br>        Chemical manufacturers<br>        Distillers<br>        Electronic engineers<br>        Foundries<br>        etc.<br>        Wholesale distributors<br>        X-ray apparatus manufacturers<br>        Yacht builders<br>        Zip fastener manufacturers<br> (ii) Institutions, schools, universities, hospitals<br>(iii) Local and Central Government The largest single group of customers<br>(iv) Agriculture |

Features differentiating these two types of market include those shown in Table 3.2.

TABLE 3.2

| Feature | Consumer markets | Industrial markets |
|---|---|---|
| 1. Buying considerations | Personal use/satisfaction/convenience, etc. | Profit<br>Cost/time savings, etc. |
| 2. Buying decisions made by: | Single individuals; at most no more than immediate members of the family circle—husband, wife, children, mother-in-law (at retail) | Single individuals, i.e. *the* Buyer Purchasing committees. Usually numerous other people participate in or influence the purchasing decision. |

TABLE 3.2 (*continued*)

| Feature | Consumer markets | Industrial markets |
|---|---|---|
| 2. (*continued*) | | They will range in status from top management to trade union representatives, and outsiders such as consultants, architects, etc.<br><br>    The exact nature of the "customer interface" is of vital importance to the sales manager in deciding upon the appropriate mix of media |
| Quality | Uninformed/ unsophisticated Amateur/irrational | Informed/expert Professional/rational (more or less) |
| 3. Number of customers | Can be numbered up to millions | Numbered in tens, hundreds, and in some cases, thousands |
| 4. Highest cost of any single purchase | Rarely ever exceeds (say) £50,000 | £1,000,000's |
| 5. Quantities | Usually singly | Frequently in bulk |
| 6. Channels of distribution | Well defined:<br>    Importer or first-hand dealer, wholesaler, retailer or multiple<br>    Independent, voluntary group or co-operative | Usually complex.<br>    Raw material extractors, shippers, brokers, converters, assemblers, contractors, dealers, etc. |
| 7. Ratio of the total volume of business | 1 | 4 times the total consumer turnover |
| 8. Geographical Distribution | Well dispersed with urban concentrations | May be highly concentrated in certain localities, i.e. certain streets in a town, certain towns in a region. This is very important in planning sales territories |

TABLE 3.2 (*continued*)

| Feature | Consumer markets | Industrial markets |
|---|---|---|
| 9. Relative importance (purchasing power) of individual customers | Each individual more or less equally important in any particular sector of a market | In any particular industry the following rule will apply: approximately 2% of customers will account for 27% of the business, 20% of the customers will account for 80% of the business, 50% of the customers will account for 97% of the business, and the other 50% of the customers for only 3% of the business |
| 10. Consumption/use of product/service | Ultimate | Intermediate—as a means to an end |
| 11. Types of product: Unfinished consumable | Food, cloth, | Raw materials |
| Semi-finished consumable | Processed convenience foods, | Components, assemblies |
| Finished consumable | Clothing, shoes, | Small tools, office supplies |
| Finished semi-durable | Furniture, appliances, | Office and engineering equipment |
| Finished durable/capital | Cars, houses, yachts | Factories, plant, ships, bridges, railways, aeroplanes, etc. |
| 12. Effect of restrictive trade practices, political and economic factors upon demand | Not critical. Consumer demand will vary seasonally, but on the whole it is fairly stable | Critical. Although industrial demand is derived from consumer demand it is generally much more sensitive. The fluctuations in demand grow greater and greater along the channels of distribution from the retail end, through to the raw material extraction end of the system |

## How, Where, When?

The answer to these three questions will be derived partly from market research. In addition, the techniques of work study and operational research will usually have to be employed.

### COMMISSIONING MARKET RESEARCH

Clearly, within the framework outlined above, there is room for enormous diversity. The problems of the individual business will be unique. Whilst every business is different, this is no excuse for saying that market research is not applicable to your own business, although it may be applicable to others. Furthermore, it is wise to do market research before—not after—investing heavily in technical research and development and manufacturing facilities.

The first and most difficult step is to recognize the existence of the suspected problem or opportunity. At this stage it will appear in very hazy outline.

The next step is a preliminary investigation to try to define the problem or opportunity more clearly. The sales or marketing manager may be able to do this himself, or may require outside help. If outside help is required, it will be readily available in the larger companies in their own market-research departments, if they possess them. Failing this, help can be obtained either from the company's advertising agency* or better still, a reputable individual or firm of management consultants* who may or may not have their own market research department. At this preliminary stage it is preferable not to go direct to an outside specialist market-research firm,* because the next stage will involve obtaining competitive proposals and cost and time quotations.

* It may be a problem to choose the best advertising agency, management consultants, or market research company for your requirements. If such is the case the following organisations can put you in touch with a short list of suitable companies:
                    Institute of Practitioners in Advertising
                    Institute of Management Consultants
                    Market Research Association.

Having narrowed down the problem or opportunity and defined it clearly, the next step is to draft the terms of reference and define the scope of the investigation to be undertaken. It is at this stage that competitive proposals for the work should be sought— usually no more than three. This should be done even if the company has its own market research department, because however competent, they may lack expertise in certain areas and, moreover, competition will be stimulating for them.

Having received and examined the competing proposals it is a good idea then to call in the firms concerned to discuss them with you. In particular you want to discuss the proposals with the individuals who would actually be doing the work in the event of your commissioning it with them.

This will help you form an opinion as to the best team to do the investigation and also to make sure that the terms of reference are clearly understood.

It then remains to authorize the investigation with the research company of your choice. Once the work is under way they should maintain close contact and inform you of progress right up to the moment they present their report. The findings should be presented to you both verbally and in the form of a written report.

The verbal presentation should be a summary of their findings, conclusions and recommendations. The written report should be in the form:

    (i)    Introduction—a brief outline of the subject.
    (ii)   Terms of reference.
    (iii)  Summary of findings, conclusions and recommendations.
    (iv)  Findings in detail.
    (v)   Arguments supporting the conclusions.
    (vi)  Recommendation in detail.
    (vii)  Appendices, tables and supporting data, etc.

In this form because, although the sales or marketing manager will be interested in every detail, other executives will usually only be concerned with the summary of findings, conclusions and recommendations.

### Example of a Market-research Brief

Here is an example of the kind of brief that a sales or marketing manager should draw up to give to market research firms, when requesting competing proposals and quotations for cost and time. This is for an industrial market survey for a firm of printers' block-makers.

#### MARKET RESEARCH PROJECT

*Objective*

To review, and forecast likely developments in the technology of, and markets for:

    (i)   Black and white, and colour printing blocks.

   (ii)   Services allied to (i).

\*(iii)   Products/processes having a common or similar technology to (i), but markets other than the printing industry.

This survey will form the basis upon which to plan the company's short/medium-term objectives and their means of achievement.

*Existing Processes/Products/Services*

1. *Process engraving*

    (i)   Black and white letterpress blocks.

   (ii)   Colour letterpress blocks.

   Markets 1, 2 and 3 below.

   (i) represents $42\frac{1}{2}\%$ and (ii) $30\%$ of the company's total turnover.

2. *Offset lithography*

    (i)   Black and white litho plates.

   (ii)   Colour litho plates.

   Markets 1, 2 and 3 below.

   (i) and (ii) combined represent $12\frac{1}{2}\%$ of the company's total turnover.

\* Low priority at the present time.

3. *Type setting and foundry*
(put out to other suppliers)
Market 1 below.
This represents 15% of the company's total turnover.

4. *Photofabrication*
A process whereby metal parts are fabricated by chemical rather than mechanical means.
Only an idea at the present time, intended for market 4 below.

*Existing Markets Served by the Company*

1. *Advertising agents*
Products/Processes/Services: 1, 2 and 3 above.
Significant features of this market appear to be that:
  (i) Price is not critical.
  (ii) The main requirements are:
     high quality;
     fast delivery—frequently overnight.
  (iii) It is sometimes difficult to identify the person(s) making or influencing the purchasing decision due to informal organization within client companies, and hence
  (iv) Personal relationships are an important factor in selling to this type of customer.
  (v) Customers tend to be very loyal to existing suppliers of colour blocks, but not black and white.
  (vi) Large agencies demand an excessive level of service.
The company is at present serving fifty-seven medium/small customers. Sales to this market represent 54% of the company's turnover.

2. *Printers*
Products/Processes/Services: 1 and 2 above. Significant features of this market appear to be that:
  (i) Printers have little loyalty to suppliers.

(ii) Although more knowledgeable than other customers, printers tend to be unbusinesslike in their relationships with suppliers.

The company is serving ninety-six printers.

Turnover amounts to 19% of the total.

3. *Publishers*

Products/Processes/Services: 1 and 2 above.

   (i) Price is critical.
  (ii) Speed of delivery is important when press date is imminent.
 (iii) Sometimes lower than average quality is acceptable at corresponding prices.
 (iv) Regular (weekly, monthly) business. This helps greatly in planning the overall workload of the plant.
  (v) Loyal to existing suppliers of colour blocks, but not black and white.

The company is serving thirty-one publishers. Turnover amounts to 21% of the total.

### *Prospective Markets*

4. *Light engineering, electronics, etc.*

Processes/Products/Services: 4 above.

Virtually nothing is known about these markets yet. The photofabrication process is suitable where there is requirement for high precision at moderate cost and/or short run production of metal components.

### WORK STUDY

In sales management work study may be used to solve the problems of How? and Where?

Work study is composed of:

   (i) *Method study*—or the examination of the ways in which jobs are carried out in order to devise better methods and thus improve performance.

(ii) *Work measurement*—or the timing of the various elements of a job in order to build up equitable work-loads.

The data derived from work study may then be used, in conjunction with that derived from market research, to:

(i) Plan sales territories with equal work-loads. Ideally the commercial potentials of territories should also be approximately equal, but this is not often possible. For example, with equal work-loads, London may have a very high potential, whereas the East Midlands may have only a moderate potential.

(ii) Plan the optimum location of sales offices, and salesmen's homes.

(iii) Plan journey cycles in sales territories.

(iv) Draw up realistic job specifications for salesmen.

As in the case of market research, the sales manager will rarely be called upon actually to conduct work study, but he would be concerned with commissioning it, and implementing the resulting recommendations.

If your company has a work-study department in the factory, enlist their aid. At first they will probably be very surprised at your request, and then delighted to have an opportunity to get out into the field. Failing this, you will have to employ outside consultants, either one of the full-service management consultants, or a firm of work-study specialists.

Again, as in the case of market research, it is essential to define the problem clearly and draw up clear terms of reference to define the scope of the investigation.

As a start, in order to see just how big the problem is, the sales manager can initiate a simple form of activity sampling. The salesmen should be asked to fill in a form noting down what they are doing at quarter-hour intervals, as near the time as possible, throughout the day for, say, one journey cycle. You will have to "sell" this to your salesmen very carefully, empha-sizing that you are not spying on them, but are doing this to help them to do their jobs better with less effort. They cannot cheat by the way, it would be far too difficult.

The result could be something like that shown in Table 3.3.

TABLE 3.3

| Activity | Code | Activity | Code |
|---|---|---|---|
| Driving | D | Service calls | C |
| Parking and walk from car at destination | P | Meals and refreshments | M |
| Waiting | W | Report writing and call preparation | R |
| Talking to customer (chat) | T | Others—specify | |
| Purposeful selling | S | | |

Salesman B. JONES    Territory: ESSEX    Area: HARLOW

| Time | Activity | Time | Activity | Time | Activity |
|---|---|---|---|---|---|
| 0800 | R | 1300 | M | 1800 | D |
| 15 | D | 15 | M | 15 | D |
| 30 | D | 30 | M | 30 | D |
| 45 | D | 45 | D | 45 | D |
| 0900 | W | 1400 | W | 1900 | M |
| 15 | S | 15 | C | 15 | M |
| 30 | S | 30 | C | 30 | M |
| 45 | D | 45 | D | 45 | M |
| 1000 | W | 1500 | D | 2000 | M |
| 15 | C | 15 | P | 15 | M |
| 30 | D | 30 | M | 30 | R |
| 45 | P | 45 | W | 45 | R |
| 1100 | T | 1600 | T | 2100 | R |
| 15 | S | 15 | S | 15 | R |
| 30 | M | 30 | S | 30 | R |
| 45 | W | 45 | C | 45 | R |
| 1200 | S | 1700 | D | 2200 | — |
| 15 | C | 15 | C | — | — |
| 30 | D | 30 | C | — | — |
| 45 | P | 45 | D | — | — |

The results will probably surprise you. They will certainly raise some interesting questions. Over a whole journey cycle they may work out like this:

*Driving:* 31% of his time was spent driving. This appears rather high. Has he planned his journeys carefully? Where does he live—is his home too far away from the majority of his customers?

*Parking:* 4% of his time was spent parking his car.

*Waiting:* 7% of his time was spent waiting to see the customer.

*Talking (chat):* 5% of his time was spent chatting, as a preliminary to purposeful selling.

These figures seem reasonable, but could he have used the waiting time for writing reports?

*Purposeful selling:* Only 16% of his time was actually spent in purposeful selling. This is what we are paying for—at this rate selling time is extremely expensive. How could he increase this—better journey planning?

A 4% increase in selling time would amount to a 25% improvement.

*Service calls:* 10% of his time was spent on service calls. This seems reasonable at the present time, but improved reliability of our product should enable this to be reduced in future.

*Meals and refreshment:* 12% of his time was spent on meals and refreshment. This seems reasonable.

*Report writing, etc.:* 15% of his time was spent on report writing and call preparation. He sits up half the night writing reports apparently. Are these necessary? What do we do with them? Time taken up in preparation and planning is well spent, but he does not appear to be doing it very effectively. Does he need training in call preparation and journey planning?

These figures should not be taken as typical by any means. In fact they will vary greatly from company to company, market to market, salesman to salesman, and territory to territory. The results you get for your own salesmen will give you very clear indications about the direction and scope of the work-study investigations that should be undertaken.

## OPERATIONAL RESEARCH

In many companies the sales manager may have responsibility for sales warehouses or depots, and their associated distributive systems.

These two operations involve several very complex problems of optimization which can only be resolved by advanced techniques of scientific investigation. Some of these techniques may also be applied in studying the operations of the sales force, but usually straightforward work study will be sufficient. The division between work study and operational research is not well defined simply because O.R. developed from the former.

The problem of holding stock is one of balancing supply against demand and striking a compromise between the standard of service desired and its associated cost.

You will want to know:

How much to order.

When to order.

How much to stock.

Demand will originate from your customers. Your delivery system will have to be organized to give an optimum speed and frequency of delivery consistent with the cost. The stock-keeping operation then has to balance the delivery schedules against supply, which may be either from your own factory(ies) or other suppliers, or both. Whoever supplies you will then have to incorporate your orders into their own production schedules.

The problem of distribution, already touched upon, is again one of giving an optimum service consistent with the cost.

You will want to know:

How many depots to have.

Where to locate them.

What types of transport to use.

The quantity of transport facilities required.

What delivery routes to use.

The optimum speed and frequency of deliveries.

These two topics will be considered further in Chapter 8.

If you have problems in these areas, except in the very biggest companies with their own O.R. departments, you will have to call upon expert outside advice.

### EMPLOYEE-ATTITUDE SURVEYS

The techniques developed by psychologists and sociologists for investigating the attitudes, behaviour and motivation of people either as voters or domestic consumers, may also be used to study the problems of employees within an organization. At the present time very few companies indeed have attempted such an investigation. Nevertheless, such studies can yield insights of great value to management and sociologist alike.

Such an investigation would cover the following aspects:

   (i)   The company as an employer in relation to others the employee has worked for or knows about.
  (ii)   The employee's particular job; the degree of satisfaction achieved; understanding of his role and function; workloads, rewards, prospects, training, etc.
 (iii)   The degree of confidence the employee has in his immediate boss.
 (iv)   Perception of and preference for managerial styles of leadership:

> hard-line authoritarian    (tells)
> benevolent authoritarian  (sells)
> consultative                    (listens)
> participative                   (joins)

It may be difficult to get acceptance of the desirability of doing such a study in the first place, particularly if the general style of management leadership is autocratic. If this difficulty can be overcome, any outside agency, such as the Tavistock Institute of Human Relations, Ashridge Management College Research Department, or one of the university sociological research departments, should be authorized to conduct the study.

REFERENCE: "The Motivation of Sales Executives in Two Major Companies", by GILLIAN PURCER SMITH, Ashridge Management College, in *British Journal of Marketing,* No. 2, Autumn 1967.

# CHAPTER 4

# FORMULATION OF POLICY

## INTRODUCTION

THE entrepreneurial or policy-making functions of general management are:

1. Forecasting
   (a) Anticipating the future effects of past and current events—the future that has already happened.
   (b) Identification of risks and opportunities.
2. Establishing objectives—the future we want to create.
3. Establishing basic operating policies—the principal means of attaining these objectives.

Thus the policy-making functions of sales management are:

1. Sales forecasting.
2. Establishing sales objectives, consistent with corporate objectives in terms of:

   quantities,
   revenue,
   profitability,
   market standing,

   by: products/services, territories and customer classification.
3. Establishing basic operating policies—Sales Strategy— consistent with the overall Marketing Communications Strategy of the company:

   The Marketing Mix—The Product/Service itself
   Pricing
   Sales Force

Packaging
Advertising
Sales Promotion
Public Relations
Warehousing and Distribution

## SALES FORECASTING

What has happened in the past cannot be undone. The present is a transitory moment. The chief concern of management is the future.

Clearly defined objectives cannot be established unless a systematic attempt has been made to foresee the future. It is true that forecasting is difficult and that forecasts are never accurate. Nevertheless, a conscientious attempt at forecasting must be made. Realistic and achievable objectives can be established even if the forecast is not of the highest order of accuracy.

It is important to distinguish between a sales forecast and a sales target. Quite often these two words are used interchangeably. The forecast is what *might* happen in the future, the target is the objective or what we actually want to happen in the future.

### Factors to Consider in Forecasting

There are numerous variable factors which can affect the future of the economy in general, and the individual business in particular. The forecaster must therefore identify which factors are likely to affect his business and the relative importance of each one. This is difficult. Some factors may be believed to have an effect to a greater or lesser degree, but on investigation turn out to have no effect at all. Other factors which have a serious effect may be overlooked. Good judgement and careful investigation are required.

The variable factors which should be considered when making a forecast include:

1. *Socio-economic factors*
   1. Population:

| | |
|---|---|
| Births | Emigration |
| Marriages | Age Distribution |
| Deaths | Geographical Distribution |
| Immigration | Minorities |

   2. Employment and Income.
   3. Consumption and Expenditure.
   4. Distribution of Goods and Services:

           Retail
           Wholesale
           Import
           Export
           Transport
           Communication
           Geographical Location
           Prices
           Finance

   5. Production of Goods and Services

           Food and Agriculture
           Building and Construction
           Fuel and Power
           Raw Materials
           Industrial/Intermediate Materials
           Finished Goods and Services
           Geographical Location.

   6. Technological innovation.
   7. Political Changes.
   8. Climate/weather.

These headings are taken from the *Annual Abstract of Statistics*.


2. *Market factors*
   1. Products, Processes or Services and their applications.
   2. Consumers/Users and their requirements.
   3. Prices and Margins.

4. Manufacturers/Supplies.
5. Distributors/Intermediaries.
6. Export/Import.
7. Volume of business in money and quantities by:

$$\left\{\begin{array}{l} \text{Products, Processes or Services} \\ \text{Consumers/Users} \\ \text{Manufacturers/Suppliers} \\ \text{Distributors/Intermediaries} \\ \text{Export/Import} \end{array}\right.$$

8. Structure of the Channels of Distribution—relationships between Eventual Consumers/Users, Manufacturers/Suppliers, Distributors/Intermediaries, etc., and any significant changes that are taking place in this structure.
9. Promotional efforts by Manufacturers/Suppliers, etc.
10. Development of New Products, Processes or Services.


3. *Internal factors*

The Company's own human, material and financial resources.


**Collection of information**

Forecasting is obviously closely related to market research. Ideally, there should be a formalized and continuous economic and market research function of the appropriate degree of sophistication in any business—large or small. All sources of relevant information should be investigated.

These will include:

*Published Information*

   (i) Government Reports and Statistics.
  (ii) Trade and Technical Press.
 (iii) Trade and Research Associations Journals.
 (iv) Chambers of Commerce Reports.

(v) Abstract Journals.

(vi) Buyers Guides.

(vii) Bankers and Stockbrokers Publications.

(viii) Subscription Services.

*Unpublished Information*

EXTERNAL SOURCES

(i) Trade and Research Associations.

(ii) National Associations (C.B.I., etc.).

(iii) Chambers of Commerce.

INTERNAL SOURCES

(i) Sales records.

(ii) Buying office.

(iii) Research and Development.

## Statistical Aids to Forecasting

### *Time Series Analysis*

On the assumption that the future follows the past with a certain measure of continuity it is possible to project the trends of past events into the future. In problems of an economic nature it has proved useful to classify trends into long-term, short-term, seasonal and random effects.

*Long-term trends.* These are the trends of events that might be called collectively "The Broad Stream of History".

*Economic cycles.* The business cycle of boom or bust. In the history of business there have apparently always been ups and downs, but there is a long-term trend superimposed on the business cycle. The period of the cycle has tended to grow shorter and the amplitude smaller. This has come about by an increased understanding of economics. At the present time the period of the cycle is about $3\frac{1}{2}$ years, and though we still have economic difficulties they are not so severe as the great crashes and booms of the past.

*Seasonal effects.* Most businesses are affected by the seasonal cycle, some more than others. It usually affects sales, and thus the income and financing of the business, and it can also affect the availability of staff, for instance.

*Random effects.* There will always be elements in any trend which are not understood and left unexplained as random effects. These effects may be large or small; if large the main weight of study should be directed to their analysis.

## Smoothing of Data

The raw data in any time series—economic statistics, past sales figures, etc.—are usually not in a form that readily lend themselves to straightforward projection into the future. They require further mathematical treatment to convert them into a conveniently usable form to make the trends explicit.

*Graphing.* Ordinary squared graph paper can be used. The raw data (sales figures) can be plotted against time. The result will be the familiar zig-zag pattern. Sometimes the trend will readily be recognizable and it can be projected into the future freehand on the graph. Plotting the raw data on semilogarithmic graph paper will also help to make the trend more explicit. Semilogarithmic graph paper has the advantage over ordinary squared paper in that it makes it easier to determine the rate of change in a trend. A straight line on squared paper indicates an increase (or decrease) at a decreasing rate, whereas a straight line on semilogarithmic paper indicates an increase (or decrease) at a steady rate.

*Moving averages.* It is usually necessary to take the moving average of raw data to make the trends more explicit. Depending on the time period used, they can identify the seasonal fluctuations (monthly moving average), the business cycle (yearly moving average) and the long-term trends (3 or 5 yearly moving average).

The moving average is simply calculated by taking an odd number (3,5,7) of periods (months, years) and finding the arithmetic mean of the values for these periods. The next average is calculated by omitting the first value included in the previous average, and including the value for the next period immediately after the last period in the previous average.

As an example let us consider the market for a product "X" from the point of view of a manufacturer delivering his own brand "Y" to the wholesale distributive trade.

The history of deliveries by *all* manufacturers, and by the manufacturers of brand "Y", to the wholesale distributive trade is as shown in Table 4.1.

TABLE 4.1

| Year | Deliveries by ALL manufacturers of product "X" '000 units | | Deliveries by manufacturer of brand "Y" of product "X" '000 units | |
|---|---|---|---|---|
| | Actual deliveries | 3-year moving average | Actual deliveries | 3-year moving average |
| 0 | N.A. | — | 10·1 | — |
| 1 | N.A. | — | 9·7 | 9·8 |
| 2 | N.A. | — | 9·5 | 10·9 |
| 3 | 178 | — | 13·5 | 13·3 |
| 4 | 210 | 240 | 17·0 | 21·0 |
| 5 | 333 | 361 | 32·4 | 30·3 |
| 6 | 539 | 478 | 41·6 | 38·6 |
| 7 | 563 | 589 | 41·7 | 44·2 |
| 8 | 666 | 753 | 49·2 | 55·6 |
| 9 | 1031 | 1032 | 76·0 | 66·7 |
| 10 | 1399 | 1214 | 74·9 | 79·6 |
| 11 | 1211 | 1331 | 87·8 | 93·3 |
| 12 | 1382 | 1597 | 117·2 | 138·0 |
| 13 | 2199 | 1733 | 209·1 | 166·3 |
| 14 | 1617 | — | 172·5 | — |

As can be seen from Fig. 4.1, plotted on ordinary squared paper, it is difficult, and it could be very misleading, to project on the likely course of wholesale demand. On Fig. 4.2, though, plotted on semilogarithmic paper, the likely course is much more obvious.

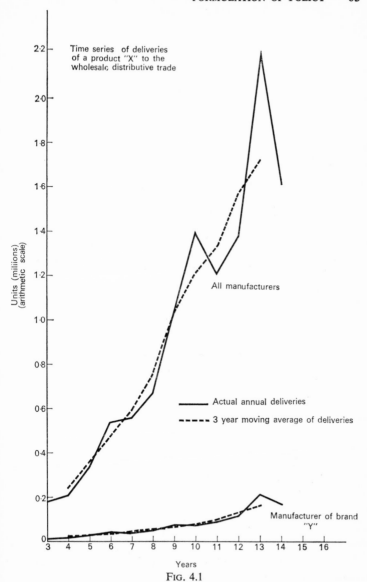

Time series of deliveries
of a product "X" to the
wholesale distributive trade

All manufacturers

Actual annual deliveries

3 year moving average of deliveries

Manufacturer of brand
"Y"

Units (millions)
(arithmetic scale)

Years

FIG. 4.1

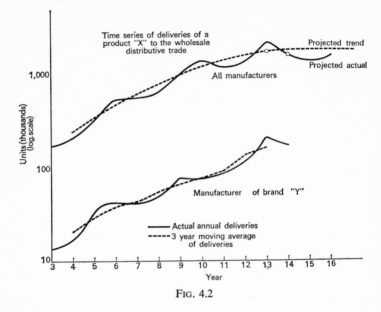

FIG. 4.2

The basic trend line made explicit by plotting the 3-year moving average can be projected on by hand. It appears that the market is, in fact, nearing saturation and the trend in the next 2 or 3 years could start to go downwards.

The wholesale demand appears to be fluctuating around the basic trend in a 3–4-year cycle.

It seems reasonable to guess therefore that next year's (year 15) demand will be down yet again, although in year 16 it will probably go up. By eye, and plotting the curve on by hand alone, it is possible to say that the demands in years 15 and 16 will be of the order of:

Year 15    —    1,400,000 units
Year 16    —    1,600,000 units

At least the manufacturer of brand "Y" is pretty certain that unless he takes countervailing measures in year 15 his sales and profits will be down still further than in year 14.

*Exponential smoothing.* This is a mathematical technique for condensing a large amount of information into a more easily handleable form. A weight $(1 - X)$ is ascribed to the average of all the past information except the most recent; and another weight $(X)$ is ascribed to the most recent piece of information. $(X)$ is less than 1. The sum of the two weighted pieces of information thus provides an exponentially smoothed average which can be used as a forecast for the next period ahead;

    i.e.   (Average of all past sales figures except the most recent)
         $\times(1-X)+$(the most recent sales figure) $\times X=$forecast sales
         for next period ahead.

If necessary, a term to take any trend into account, can be added.

The value of $(X)$ is chosen according to the degree of sensitivity required. If the formula is required to reveal the basic trend and be insensitive to short-term fluctuations, then $(X)$ should be small, say, 0·1. If, on the other hand, it is required to predict short term fluctuations, then $(X)$ should be given a larger value.

This is a strictly mechanical formula for projecting past sales figures into the future. Nevertheless, it is very useful for sales forecasting where a large number of products are being handled, such as in retail and wholesale distribution, and in particular where stocks are being controlled by computer.

In general, it should be remembered that the time series analysis approach to forecasting assumes that all the factors that have to be considered remain the same. It is thus an "all other things being equal" approach. Nevertheless it is a technique that can give a reliable and useful indication of the way sales will develop in the future, particularly in the consumable and consumer durable manufacturing industries and distributing trades.

## Indicators

There are three types of indicator which can be useful to the forecaster. There are indicators of the economy generally; and indicators specific to a particular business can usually be found.

*Leading indicators.* The most important leading indicator is the birth rate—the future that has already happened. All the children born today will be needing clothes, prams and toys in the next year or so. They will be needing education—with all that implies—between 5 and 20 years hence. Then they will get married and need housing, furniture, etc. Other valuable leading indicators are the retail price index, manufacturers' new orders, new construction starts, new businesses registered, new power (coal, oil, gas, electricity) installations.

*Coincident indicators.* These are indicators which move with the economy generally or company sales in particular. They tend to reinforce current estimates of business conditions. Such indicators of a general economic nature are the rate of employment/unemployment, index of industrial production, and retail sales.

*Lagging indicators.* These are indicators which follow the trends of the economy or company sales and will tend to confirm whether previous forecasts were correct. General economic indicators include values of manufacturers' inventories, hire purchase debt, bank rate, etc.

## Correlation

The indicators mentioned above can provide a very good general picture of how the economy as a whole and specific markets in particular are behaving. Sometimes, however, it is possible to find economic and market indicators which have a measurable relationship to the performance of a particular business.

There are various ways of discovering how suitably smoothed time series of data are correlated. Simple tabulation may be quite sufficient. Graphical methods may be used; more complicated correlations can be treated algebraically. A coefficient of the correlation can be calculated. When there is perfect positive correlation its value is $+1$, and when there is perfect negative correlation its value is $-1$.

Correlation is a purely statistical operation which can be applied to any data, but it must not be assumed too readily that a correlation indicates a cause or effect relationship. For forecasting purposes it is ideal if a leading indicator with a provable cause and effect relationship can be found.

## Econometric Models

This is a highly sophisticated approach to forecasting. It is an attempt to devise a mathematical formula or model which will predict the future behaviour of the variable under investigation by relating it to a number of other economic variables in a provable cause and effect relationship. Again, the sales manager is not expected to be able to construct econometric models. But he should have some ideas about the likely causes that affect his sales. Having postulated the likely causes, the sales manager can then leave it to the statisticians to test these hypotheses and devise the model.

## Conclusion

It should be remembered that whilst these techniques, and even more sophisticated ones developed from them, are "scientific", they are not infallible. There are too many imponderable factors to take into account. Forecasting must, therefore, remain an art and ultimately rely on judgement. Nevertheless, the power of human judgement in forecasting can be refined by adopting a systematic method. Forecasting requires good techniques, good judgement and, above all, good luck.

### ESTABLISHING OBJECTIVES

Determining the objectives of a business enterprise is the key function of management. It is an extremely difficult task and requires educated judgement of the very highest order. It requires judgement because on the one hand we have to assimilate vast amounts of information—far more than any computer ever conceived could digest—and, on the other hand, we have to make assumptions where factual information is just not available.

In determining objectives we have to consider:

1. *The external environment beyond our control:*
    (i) The natural, cultural, political, economic, legal, social and technological environment generally.
    (ii) Markets in general—consumer, industrial, domestic and overseas.
    (iii) The particular market(s) the company exists to serve— distributive channels, competitor's strengths and weaknesses, individual customers,

and ask the questions:

    (i) "Where do we stand in relation to our environment, now, at this point in time?"
    (ii) "What changes in our environment are likely to take place in the future and how will they affect us?"

2. *The means available to us within our control:*
    (i) Human resources—quantity and quality, know-how, skills, talents, abilities, strengths and weaknesses.
    (ii) Material resources—property, plant, machinery, raw materials, work in progress, finished goods.
    (iii) Financial resources—cash, credit, debtors, loans, equity.
    (iv) External communications:

> Products/Services
> Prices
> Sales Force
> Advertising
> Packaging
> Sales Promotion
> Public Relations
> Distribution

and then ask the following questions:

   (i) "With these means available to us, where can we go, and how far within a specified time in the future, from where we stand now?"

  (ii) "Could we improve upon the utilization of our resources, and thus get even further?"

 (iii) "Could we get even further still with additional resources, and if so what do we need?"

It is vitally important that a conscientious attempt is made to answer these questions, and having initiated it, to strive to reach a consensus amongst the executives concerned.

Inevitably there will be much argument and many genuine differences of opinion. This is perfectly natural, but the argument and discussion must be disinterested and impartial and not allowed to become emotional, irrational, or personal.

The importance of achieving executive consensus about the company's objectives cannot be overstated. When they are made explicit and communicated to the other people in the organization, many incalculable benefits are realized:

they provide the basis for planning, implementation and control of operations;

they provide the criteria for making decisions;

they produce consistency in decentralization and delegation of authority and responsibility;

they provide direction and purpose to the members of the organization.

In short, determination, clear definition and communication of the company's objectives disentangles all the "political" knots.

The particular responsibilities of the sales or marketing executive in determining the company's objectives are:

   (i) The identification, definition and description of the market(s) the company exists to serve.

  (ii) The standing within, or share of, each market that is to be achieved.

    (iii) The revenue, or sales turnover, that is to be achieved.

    (iv) The quantities of product(s)/service(s) that are to be sold.

    (v) The contribution that is to be made to cover establishment costs and produce a profit.

These objectives can then be further subdivided, according to the particular circumstances of the individual company by:

> products or services, either individually or in groups,
> geographical location,
> customer, market or industry classification,
> sales territories,
> individual salesmen,

either singly or in any combination.

## ESTABLISHING BASIC OPERATING POLICIES

### The Marketing Mix

A business enterprise has several alternative means at its disposal to communicate with its market. They can be used singly or in any combination. Having defined the market the company exists to serve and its marketing objectives, we have to decide upon the appropriate mixture of media to use to communicate with it. They will include:

> The Product/Service itself
> Pricing
> Sales Force
> Packaging
> Advertising
> Sales Promotion
> Public Relations and Editorial Publicity
> Warehousing and Distribution

In deciding upon the mixture, we have to identify, with the aid of market research, all the people that have to be influenced to get the product or service into use or consumption. That is, we have to identify the "customer interface".

The customer interface will differ greatly from market to market, industry to industry, and individual customer to customer. Nevertheless, in any particular section of business the customer interface will show many common features. This is very fortunate, because otherwise we would have to communicate with each individual personally.

## Customer Interface Examples

TABLE 4.2. A Manufacturer of Low-priced High-turnover Consumer Goods

Customer Interface

| People to be influenced | Means at manufacturer's disposal |
|---|---|
| 1. Individual consumer | National press and TV advertising; weekly and monthly journal and local press advertising; packaging; point of sale display; retail demonstrations; incentive promotions; posters; exhibitions; editorial publicity; direct mail; radio advertising. |
| 2. Retail shop assistant | Briefing by company's retail salesman/merchandiser; cash or prize incentive. |
| 3. Retail shop owner/manager | Company's retail salesmen/merchandiser; stocking bonus; point of sale material; trade press advertising; direct mail; cash or prize incentive. |
| 4. Wholesaler's salesman | Briefing by company's wholesale salesman, cash or prize incentive. |
| 5. Wholesaler's buyer | Company's wholesale salesman; stocking bonus; trade press advertising; direct mail; cash or prize incentive, company's delivery system, order clerk, telephonist; editorial publicity. |
| 6. Multiple, co-operative and voluntary group senior buyers/ merchandising executives | Key account sales executive; and as for wholesaler's buyer. |
| 7. Top management of 6 above | Company's senior executives; trade press advertising; editorial publicity. |

Table 4.2 represents just about the full promotional armoury that could be used. Again, it requires judgement and, if possible, a carefully controlled experiment, to decide upon the appropriate mixture. The circumstances will differ in each case and it may not be necessary to go to the extent of employing four distinct sales forces—retail demonstrators, retail salesmen/merchandisers, wholesale salesmen and key account sales executives—for instance. Naturally, if more than one sales force is employed, the job of managing each one will be different. They will also differ greatly in character.

TABLE 4.3. A Manufacturer of Industrial Power Tools
(or any Production Line Equipment)

Customer Interface

| People to be influenced | Means at manufacturer's disposal |
| --- | --- |
| 1. Prime purchasing decision-maker(s):<br>(a) Small company: owner/general manager.<br>(b) Medium-sized company: the board and works management.<br>(c) Large company: production director and his production advisory committee, production engineering consultant, works management and buyer who actually places order.<br>2. End users—operatives and maintenance people, works consultative committee who will have to agree on productivity standards, etc. | Sales engineer;<br>Trade press advertising;<br>Editorial publicity;<br>Institutional journals;<br>Direct mail;<br>Sales brochures;<br>Films;<br>Exhibitions;<br>Demonstration van tours;<br>Open days;<br>Lectures, seminars;<br>Give aways—for end users;<br>Meetings with trade unions;<br>General P.R. activity. |
| 3. Customer's top management—to ensure that company's standing and reputation is known.<br>4. Customer's employees who indirectly help sales by minimising wasted sales visits, etc., e.g. commissionaires, and secretaries who make appointments for technical sales engineer. | To 1, 2, 3 and 4: corporate advertising to generate overall awareness of company's standing; P.R. in financial area and product publicity; all forms of media, especially national and local press, and where greater area penetration is required, local TV advertising. |

TABLE 4.4. A Manufacturer of Electronic/Computers

Customer Interface

| People to be influenced | Means at manufacturer's disposal |
|---|---|
| 1. Programmers<br>Systems analysts | Teams consisting of: |
| 2. Data processing managers | Programmers (senior and junior)<br>Systems Analysts (senior and junior) |
| 3. Consultants | Salesmen (senior and junior)<br>Application specialists |
| 4. Departmental line managers | Customer classification specialists<br>Also P.R. and board level contact. |
| 5. Board—top management | |

Note: these teams are not rigidly structured, but form and reform as the occasion demands.

(Table 4.5 follows on page 74.)

TABLE 4.5. A Pharmaceutical Drug Manufacturer

| Customer Interface | |
|---|---|
| People to be influenced | Means at manufacturer's disposal |
| 1. General public (patients) | Association of British Pharmaceutical Industries; P.R. (A.B.P.I.) films; lay press (institutional) advertising; editorial publicity; exhibitions and trade shows. |
| 2. General medical practitioners | Detail men; professional journal advertising; A.B.P.I. publications; samples; symposia, conferences; exhibitions; direct mail; presentation items, diaries, calendars, etc. |
| 3. Retail, wholesale and multiple distributors (similar to example in table 4.2) | Detail men—direct selling; professional journal and trade press advertising; point of sale display; bonus offers, promotions, etc.; direct mail; company's delivery system, telephonist, order clerks, etc. |
| 4. Consultant physicians | Similar to 2 above. |
| 5. Hospital staff (nurses and laboratory people) | Detail men, factory tours; presentation items; films, etc. |
| 6. Medical students | Conferences; seminars; films; outings. |
| 7. Hospital boards | Detail men; area sales manager, factory tours, etc. |
| 8. Ministry of Health | A.B.P.I.; company's scientific/medical department; conferences; factory visits; films, etc. |
| 9. Individual M.P.'s and the Government generally | A.B.P.I.; general P.R. activity conferences, etc. |

TABLE 4.6. A Manufacturer of Fine Chemicals for Industrial Uses

Customer Interface

| People to be influenced | Means at manufacturer's disposal |
|---|---|
| 1. Buyer (usually non-technical) | *Non-technical salesman; trade press; direct mail; sales office manager; telephonist delivery service. |
| 2. Production, research and development management; quality control department. | *Non-technical salesman; sales office technical adviser; production, research and development management; quality control department; trade press; professional journals; direct mail; editorial publicity. |
| 3. Senior management | Senior management; sales manager, editorial publicity, prestige advertising. |

*Non-technical salesman employed as an "ambassador". All technical problems referred, in the first instance, to sales office technical adviser. If he cannot help, then the problem is referred to the appropriate expert in production or R. & D. This is because the range of chemicals made, and their applications, are so great, that not even a technically qualified salesman could possibly be knowledgeable about them all.

(Table 4.7 follows on page 76)

TABLE 4.7. A Newspaper Proprietor selling Classified
Advertising Space

Customer Interface

| People to be influenced | Means at disposal |
| --- | --- |
| 1. Personnel directors/managers | Personal calls by classified advertising salesman; trade press advertising. |
| 2. Personnel officers (principal buyers) | As above; and telephonists. |
| 3. Line managers employing staff | Telephonists. |
| 4. Advertising agents | Advertising agency salesmen. |
| 5. Job prospects | Poster advertising; trade and Sunday press advertising; direct mail. |
| 6. Senior level management consultants | Sales management and board contact. |
| 7. Consultants | Classified advertising salesmen. |
| 8. Incoming business | Telephonists. |
| 9. Trade associations | Management; trade press; journalists. |
| 10. Property agents, developers, etc. | Property advertising salesmen. |
| 11. Travel firms, associations | Classified advertising salesmen. |
| 12. Retailers | Classified advertising salesmen; telephone sales girls. |

TABLE 4.8. A Manufacturer of Exterior Decorative/Protective
Paints

| Customer Interface | |
| --- | --- |
| People to be influenced | Means at manufacturer's disposal |
| 1. Householders | National and local advertising; advice/information service (by post); demonstration service. |
| 2. Industrial Property Owners | Salesmen; sales manager (depending on who it is to be influenced); sales literature; sample work undertaken; photographs of other work. |
| 3. Decorators | Technical/demonstration representative; trade shows; literature; national advertising; advice/information service (personal call and by post); complaints section. |
| 4. Retail stockists | Salesmen; literature; national advertising; film shows. |
| 5. Industrial building consortia | Salesmen; technical representatives; sales manager; literature; local advertising; photographs; dinners for directors; sample work; research done. |
| 6. Builders merchants and their salesmen | Salesmen; evening lectures/films; national and local advertising; advice/information service (personal and postal); literature. |
| 7. Architects | Special architect representative; photographic aids; receptions; film shows; sample work; visits to works; golf matches. |
| 8. Local authorities<br>County and city architects/engineers<br>Job architects<br>Housing managers | Special architect representatives; sales manager at top level; evening lectures/demonstrations; technical salesmen; research; literature; sample work; golf matches; advice/information service. |

TABLE 4.9. A Distributor of Truck Tyres to Commercial Users

Customer Interface

| People to be influenced | Means at distributor's disposal |
|---|---|
| 1. Small fleet owner | Local branch manager/salesman. |
| 2. Transport manager and purchasing officer of large fleet users. | Divisional manager; local branch manager/salesman. |
| 3. Local government and nationalized industries | By tender: national accounts salesman. |
| 4. Tyre manufacturers' representative (for information and assistance) | Local branch manager. |
| 5. All fleet users | Transport journal advertising; direct mail. |

Numerous other examples to those shown in Tables 4.2–4.9 of customer interface could be given. Clearly, the kinds of customer interface must be as diverse as the whole of the business universe itself. The role and character of the sales force must therefore be equally diverse.

The basic operating policy decision about the appropriate mixture of communications media to use, in general, and the nature of the sales force in particular must, therefore, be made according to the circumstances in each individual case.

# CHAPTER 5

# PLANNING THE OPERATIONS OF THE SALES FORCE

## INTRODUCTION

HAVING decided upon the use of a sales force as one of the components of the appropriate mixture of media to communicate with the market(s) the company serves, the next step is to plan in detail the work to be done in pursuit of the objectives already established.

As we have seen in the previous chapter, because of the enormous diversity of "customer interface"—the people that have to be influenced, and the variety of possible media mixtures—the means available to do so, there can be no stereotype marketing organization, and indeed no "typical" salesman.

The structure of organizations has been the subject of much study. Many people have tried to determine sets of general rules for organizational planning, and there has been no end of theoretical speculation. Some people see the "right" organization structure as being the key to management. It is not; it is merely the framework. The organization structure is not an end in itself; it is but the means of achieving predetermined ends.

Although this work has yielded some insights of very great value, much of it remains inconclusive. We are not very much nearer to formulating a set of infallible general purpose rules for organizational planning than when we started.

However, it can be said that unless:

   (i) corporate, departmental and individual objectives are clearly defined and communicated;

  (ii) responsibility (and the requisite authority) for the achievement of results is delegated as widely as possible;

(iii)   the people to whom power has been delegated are capable of exercising it, and believe that what they are doing is worthwhile,

any organization structure will do.


## THE MARKETING ORGANIZATION

The first step in marketing/sales organizational planning is to draw up a schedule of existing and potential customers indicating:

   (i)   their industrial/trade classifications;

  (ii)   the product(s)/service(s) they are, or could be, buying;

 (iii)   the actual and potential volume of business that is being, or could be, achieved;

 (iv)   their geographical locations.

Clearly, this pattern will be unique to any individual company, but it is possible to make some generalizations.

A study of item (iii) in this schedule, the actual and potential volume of business, will show, for instance, that:

approximately $2\%$ of the customers could produce $30\%$ of the total volume;

approximately $5\%$ of the customers could produce $46\%$ of the total volume;

approximately $10\%$ of the customers could produce $65\%$ of the total volume;

approximately $50\%$ of the customers could produce $97\%$ of the total volume;

and the other $50\%$ of the customers could produce only $3\%$ of the total volume.

This analysis will help in deciding which existing or potential customers you should continue to deal with or solicit for business, and which accounts should either be closed or served by some other means, or not solicited for business at all.

All this information is required in order to plan:

the marketing/sales organization structure;

sales territories, their business potentials and work loads;

salesmen's job specifications;

the distributive network.

All marketing/sales organizations, despite the great diversity, must accommodate the four basic dimensions of marketing activity; the various marketing functions, customer classifications, products/services, and regions/areas/territories, as indicated above.

The appropriate organization structure must, of course, be designed to suit the purposes and circumstances of the individual company. The relative importance of these four dimensions will vary. Generally speaking, however, there are four distinct types of marketing organization in which the individual sales manager may find himself.

These are:

the functionally orientated;

the customer classification orientated;

the product/service orientated;

the regionally orientated;

or various combinations of these four types.

## The Functionally Orientated Marketing Organization

This is perhaps the most common type of organization, examples of which are shown in Fig. 5.1(a)–(b).

FIG. 5.1. Typical of many small/medium-sized companies

FIG. 5.1. Wide span of control, large company

FIG. 5.1. Narrow span of control, large company

## The Customer-classification Orientated Marketing Organization

Where the customers of the company fall into distinct classifications in terms of their industry or trade, buying habits, etc., it may be desirable to organize accordingly (see Fig. 5.2(a)–(b)).

Salesmen Customer Classification A    Salesmen Customer Classification B

FIG. 5.2. Small/medium-sized company

FIG. 5.2. Large company

## The Product/Service Orientated Marketing Organization

In the case of a company producing a wide range of products, it may be desirable to construct the organization around product groups (see Fig. 5.3(a)–(c)).

(a)

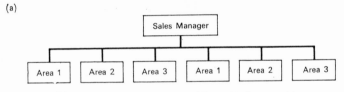

FIG. 5.3. Small/medium-sized company

(b)

FIG. 5.3. Large company, product divisions

(c)

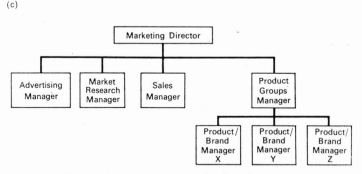

FIG. 5.3. Large company, product/brand managers

## The Regionally Orientated Marketing Organization

Companies operating over wide areas will nearly always require to organize regionally. The sales force is typically organized in this way, in addition to any customer classification or product/ service specialization, as indicated in the previous examples.

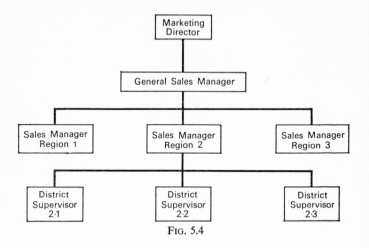

FIG. 5.4

These four organizational types have various advantages and disadvantages, which can be summarized as shown in Table 5.1.

TABLE 5.1

| Operational Characteristics | Functionally orientated | Customer classification orientated | Product/ service orientated | Regionally orientated |
|---|---|---|---|---|
| Personnel development | Fair | Poor | Excellent | Poor |
| Co-ordination of activities | Fair-poor | Good | Excellent | Poor |
| Avoidance of duplication | Good | Fair | Poor | Good |
| Utilization of advanced techniques | Excellent | Fair | Fair | Poor |
| Clear responsibility for profitability | Poor | Good | Excellent | Poor |
| Ease of understanding by employees | Fair | Good | Excellent | Excellent |

This list can be expanded, and there may be some disagreement about the ratings. Generally speaking, the greater the degree of specialization of individual effort, the less easy it is to co-ordinate activities, to pin-point responsibility and to develop all-round abilities, but the easier it is to avoid duplication and make use of advanced techniques. The specialist tends to lose sight of the grand design and to regard his own activities as ends in themselves. On the other hand, producing able all-rounders by giving them clear responsibility for achieving results and exposing them to a wide variety of experience also has its disadvantages. There is a tendency to develop too many Chiefs, but not enough Indians. In these circumstances, if there are insufficient prospects for advancement, there is likely to be a lot of frustration and a high rate of staff turnover.

## THE SALESMAN'S JOB

Having decided upon the appropriate organization structure we now have to turn our attention to the job the salesman has to do. Again there is a great diversity, but seven general types of selling job have been identified.

1. *Van selling.* This job is principally one of taking orders, delivering the goods from a van and collecting money. The amount of "selling" required is minimal.

2. *Retail selling.* Again the "selling" element is low in this type of job. It is a matter of serving a customer who has already decided to buy.

3. *Staple commodity selling.* This job requires more "selling", but is mainly a matter of collecting orders for delivery later.

4. *Ambassadorial selling.* The "selling" element in this job is quite high. Such a salesman is more of a propagandist, and does not actually take orders. An example is the building materials salesman persuading architects to specify his product(s) in their designs; or another is the pharmaceutical "detailman" who persuades doctors to prescribe his company's drugs.

In the case of the chemical company's salesman mentioned earlier, he is selling the services of his company as suppliers of chemicals and technical expertise in general rather than specific chemical products.

5. *Technical selling.* Again the "selling" element is quite high in this type of job, and it is coupled with expert technical knowledge. Such a salesman is also a consultant to his customers.

6. *Speciality selling* of tangible products. The "selling" element here is very high, and this kind is sometimes referred to as "creative" selling. The salesman here has a double role—to reveal an unrecognized, or unconscious need to the prospect, and then to sell his particular proposition.

7. *Speciality selling* of *in*tangible services. The "selling" element is even greater in this type of job since the ideas or services being sold are usually difficult for the prospect to comprehend.

All these selling jobs will have many elements in common, and could include:

*Knowledge of:*

  (i)   the company, its operations, policies and procedures;
  (ii)  the company's product(s)/service(s), their values and the markets for them;
  (iii) the company's competitors and their operations, product(s)/service(s), etc.;
  (iv)  the principles, methods and psychology of selling.

*Attitudes:*

  (i)   the necessity for selling in a free economy;
  (ii)  the will to succeed in a selling career;
  (iii) human understanding (empathy).

*Planning of:*

  (i)   work content—calls, routes and programmes;
  (ii)  approach and tactics in individual sales interviews;
  (iii) effective use of time.

*Implementation:*

  The selling process

  (i)   overcoming obstacles to the sales interview;

(ii)   opening the sales interview—identification of the main interests/problems of the customer in respect of a specific product/service;

(iii)  presentation of the case for buying—satisfaction of those interests/problems with appropriate benefits/solutions;

(iv)   negotiation—anticipating, overcoming and capitalizing upon objections to a sale;

(v)    closing the sale;

(vi)   handling complaints;

(vii)  keeping the customer sold.

In addition to this main task, there will be other elements, some regular, others irregular, such as:

travelling—driving;
waiting to see customers;
administration—report writing, planning;
service calls;
meals and refreshment;
attending sales conferences and meetings;
training—of himself and/or others;
making authorized surveys of customers requirements;
preparing formal written sales proposals;
conducting lectures and seminars;
attending exhibitions and outside conferences;
entertaining customers,
etc.

Needless to say, because of the great diversity, the requirements of each sales job have to be studied individually. No two jobs are ever the same.

## TERRITORY PLANNING

Apart from the retail salesman (2) above, most salesmen will have specific responsibilities for areas or territories.

Various approaches to the problem of territory planning have been suggested. They all have various advantages and disadvantages, and none of them represent the final solution. In any case, the information contained in the schedule mentioned on page 80 is a pre-requisite. Perhaps the most satisfactory approach is the one which attempts to measure and equalize the territorial work loads of individual salesmen and then, so far as is possible, to balance the territorial sales potentials. If one approaches it the other way round—to equalize territorial sales potential first— the work loads are likely to be very disparate and unfair.

The work load approach, however, rests upon one critical decision, and that is the appropriate call frequency. Usually this is chosen quite arbitrarily:

| | | |
|---|---|---|
| e.g. | high-potential customers | once a week |
| | good-potential customers | once a fortnight |
| | moderate-potential customers | once a month |
| | low-potential customers | once a quarter |

It must be made clear, though, that there can be no absolutely "right" call frequency. Ideally, carefully controlled experiments should be carried out to determine the effects on sales of different call frequencies in different territories—bearing in mind that the effects will change with time. They will also change according to other changes made in the media mix—price, quality, advertising and sales promotion, etc., changes occurring in the economy generally and in competitive activity. Ultimately you will have to rely on your own judgement.

Having decided upon the appropriate call-frequency for different categories of customer, the next step is to measure the number of calls a salesman can make in a specific period of time— per week or per month, for instance. This will depend upon the particular selling job he has to do. As indicated earlier, each selling job can be broken down into its elements. Some elements will be regular and others irregular. The amount of time spent performing each activity can be measured either by a simple form of activity sampling, or more sophisticated work-study techniques.

One of the largest elements will be the time spent in travelling or driving, and this will depend upon the geographical location of customers and the terrain generally—town or country, population density and availability and quality of road, rail or air transport facilities.

Planning journeys within a territory in order to minimize the time spent travelling can be an extremely complex task. However, this is no excuse for not trying. At least, the customers should be plotted on a map. If this has never been done before, it could, by itself, suggest different and better ways of covering the territory. The next step is to try to build up journeys by making string diagrams on the map. This is not so easy. To see how difficult it is, stick some pins into a piece of cardboard as shown in Fig. 5.5, and then join them up, from home to home, with a piece of string or cotton. Try, say, ten different patterns and measure the total length of string, making a note of the order in which the pins have been covered, on each occasion.

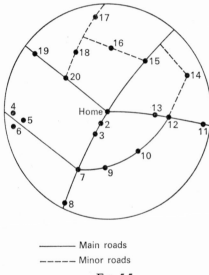

——————— Main roads
– – – – – Minor roads

FIG. 5.5

It will be realized that to carry out a similar exercise on a real territory with major and minor roads, congested urban areas and traffic-free country areas, and customers who have to be called upon at different frequencies, is an extremely complex task indeed. More advanced techniques of simulation need to be used to find the "best" way to cover the territory. The problem of devising vehicle-delivery routes is, of course, the same.

Having measured, as well as is practically possible, the average length of time of each sales interview—which will, in most cases, be approximately the same throughout, the time spent in travelling—which will vary greatly from one part of the country to another, and the other occasional elements; we can then calculate the average number of calls each salesman should be able to achieve, say, per week, according to the nature of the terrain in the different areas.

From this figure we can then calculate the number of salesmen required.

Let us consider a simple example, illustrating this approach. Say we have

Class A1: 75 Urban $\Big\}$ high-potential customers to be called
 A2: 25 Country $\Big\}$ upon once a week
 B1: 200 Urban $\Big\}$ good-potential customers to be called
 B2: 300 Country $\Big\}$ upon once a fortnight
 C1: 500 Urban $\Big\}$ moderate-potential customers to be
 C2: 500 Country $\Big\}$ called upon once a month

and the salesmen can make calls at the rate of 160 a month in urban areas and 120 a month in country areas.

The total number of calls required per month

$$= (75 \times 4 + 200 \times 2 + 500) + (25 \times 4 + 300 \times 2 + 500)$$

$$= 1200 \text{ urban} + 1200 \text{ country calls}$$

therefore, the number of salesmen required

$$= \frac{1200}{160} + \frac{1200}{120}$$

$$= 18 \text{ salesmen}$$

In order to allocate equal work load territories to each of the 18 salesmen, the map should be ruled up into, say 20 mile squares. Each square should show the information given in Table 5.2.

TABLE 5.2

| Number of Customers | Number of calls per month | Time required |
|---|---|---|
| No. of A1 | No. of A1 × 4 | No. of A1 × 4 × $\dfrac{1}{160}$ of a month |
| A2 | A2 × 4 | A2 × 4 × $\dfrac{1}{120}$ |
| B1 | B1 × 2 | B1 × 2 × $\dfrac{1}{160}$ |
| B2 | B2 × 2 | B2 × 2 × $\dfrac{1}{120}$ |
| C1 | C1 × 1 | C1 × 1 × $\dfrac{1}{160}$ |
| C2 | C2 × 1 | C2 × 1 × $\dfrac{1}{120}$ |
| | Total time required: | a fraction of a month |

Then, by inspection, clusters of squares should be chosen to form territories in such a way that each cluster is as compact as possible and contains approximately one month's work. The business potential of each territory can then be calculated by reference to the schedule of customers already prepared.

Although this approach is straightforward enough, it is a laborious and time-consuming exercise to carry out. Like all other management problems, there are no simple formulae or short-cuts. Each problem has to be considered individually according to the circumstances.

### THE JOB SPECIFICATION

Having studied the requirements of the job to be done in detail and planned the territory the salesman is to operate in, it is then possible to draw up a job specification or description, which should include:

The objectives of the job.
Quantitative sales targets.
Lists of customers.

Work loads.

Precise delineation of territory.

Responsibilities and authority.

Duties in detail, including:

    (i) Organization of the work.

    (ii) Knowledge of the company's product(s)/service(s), customers, markets, policies, procedures, terms, competitors, etc.

    (iii) Selling principles and techniques.

    (iv) Relationships with colleagues and internal staff.

    (v) Relationships with customers and other outside individuals and organizations.

    (vi) Training requirements.

    (vii) Care of the company's property—car, sales aids, etc.

    (viii) Dealing with complaints.

    (ix) Reports.

The importance of having a realistic written job specification cannot be overstated, since it is the key to the management of the sales force in the field. It enables the sales manager to recruit the right kind of men, to appraise their performance, to decide upon the nature and scope of training required, to delegate and co-ordinate work and responsibility, and to direct, motivate and control the sales force.

### THE MAN PROFILE

The next question that has to be answered is: "What is the right kind of man to do the job?"

The salesman is a very expensive member of any company's staff. The total cost of employing him should be related to the amount of time he actually spends face to face with his customers —his really productive work. On this basis, his time is at least as expensive as that of top management. If he leaves the company he is very expensive to replace. If he is not the right man and his performance is poor in relation to the potential, then he is extremely expensive indeed.

Many people have tried to find the magical mixture of personal qualities that make a successful salesman. Some even claim to have discovered it! However, since there is such a diversity and selling jobs differ so much, there can be no "typical" or "ideal" salesman.

The kind of salesman for your company will depend upon the nature of the job you have just specified, which itself will depend upon the company's own particular circumstances and goals. Deciding upon the appropriate mixture of personal qualities is very much a matter of judgement. Whereas the measurement and specification of the job to be done is more or less a straight-forward mechanical procedure, deciding upon the kind of man to do the job can never be a matter of applying a routine formula.

All that can be offered to help the sales manager decide this very difficult question is a framework for judgement.

Initially, you will have to make some fairly arbitrary guesses about the qualifications and qualities that are required for the job specified. Then you can think them over and ask yourself "why?" in each case. Having done this, and probably modified your original ideas considerably, you can then draw up your "ideal" man profile, with allowable variances from the ideal. If you do this really carefully and conscientiously, you will not be far out in your assessment. Later on, when you come to measuring the salesmen's performance, you may have to modify your ideas yet again. This time, though, you will be able to reach an even closer approximation to the ideal, because you will be starting from a set of well-thought-out premises. Still later on, when the circumstances of the job itself may have changed considerably, you will have to start all over again.

You can draw up a chart, as an aid to judgement, as shown in Table 5.3. There can be much argument about these factors.

## Qualifications

*Age.* Usually a lower age limit is set because the man could not have acquired sufficient experience. A higher age limit has to be set for a variety of reasons, such as the company's

TABLE 5.3

**Man Profile**

| Qualifications | Undesirable | Why? | Essential | Why? | Acceptable | Why? | Ideally desirable | Why? |
|---|---|---|---|---|---|---|---|---|
| Age | | | | | | | | |
| Male or female | | | | | | | | |
| Education | | | | | | | | |
| Marital status/family | | | | | | | | |
| Health | | | | | | | | |
| Interests | | | | | | | | |
| Previous employment/ sales experience | | | | | | | | |
| Nationality | | | | | | | | |
| Location | | | | | | | | |
| Car driver | | | | | | | | |
| References | | | | | | | | |
| Others (specify) | | | | | | | | |

| | | | | | | |
|---|---|---|---|---|---|---|
| Appearance | | | | | | |
| Manner/social qualities | | | | | | |
| Human understanding (empathy) | | | | | | |
| Persuasiveness | | | | | | |
| Articulation | | | | | | |
| Intelligence | | | | | | |
| Initiative | | | | | | |
| Independence | | | | | | |
| Ambition | | | | | | |
| Enthusiasm | | | | | | |
| Patience | | | | | | |
| Judgement | | | | | | |
| Creativity | | | | | | |
| Integrity | | | | | | |
| Loyalty | | | | | | |
| Others (specify) | | | | | | |

pension scheme not allowing entrants over a certain age. Make sure the reasons for setting the upper limit are strictly valid, because you might otherwise exclude some first-rate people out of work, particularly in these days of take-overs, through no fault of their own.

*Male or female.* Do not automatically exclude the fair sex. They may be ideal in certain jobs and far better than their male counterparts.

*Education.* Remember that the salesman is essentially a persuasive communicator—so his command of his native language is the most important factor. High academic or professional qualifications are only necessary for the consultant type of salesman, and even then he should not be too highly specialized. He should be able to call upon specialist expertise from within the company.

*Marital status.* There is no conclusive evidence that a married man works better than a single one, nor that a happily married man works better than an unhappily married man. If a high degree of mobility is required, then a single man is preferable. Remember that a man's wife is also an unpaid secretary. In certain cases, particularly overseas, a lot of business is conducted on the social round, so it helps if a man's wife is a good hostess.

*Health.* Must be sound, mentally and physically. Sometimes minor disabilities, such as mild colour blindness, will exclude.

*Interests.* All work and no play makes Jack a dull boy. Exclude certain types of very time-consuming hobbies and interests. Sometimes, though, time-consuming activities, such as local politics, can be very advantageous.

*Previous employment/sales experience.* Remember that experienced men may think they "know it all", and therefore require re-training. They will want more money than novices. Inexperienced men will require training.

*Nationality.* Some people believe that only a Welshman can sell to a Welshman, an Irishman to an Irishman, and a

Scotsman to a Scotsman. Maybe this is true, but remember that they may get too involved with the social round.

*Location.* On the territory already, or willing to move.

*Car driver.* Three endorsements on his driving license will exclude. Membership of one of the advanced driving associations is advantageous; you may be able to get reduced insurance rates.

*References.* Sometimes of doubtful value. Only approach his present employer after you have offered him the job.

## Personal Qualities

The trouble with these personal qualities is that they are very subjective. They are usually difficult to define and almost impossible to measure. Nevertheless it is possible to gain impressions about their presence, and in what degree, and thus to form opinions about the standards desirable.

*Appearance.* This will depend to a large extent upon your own standards, but remember the kind of people he will be dealing with. A black jacket and pin-stripes may be just as out of place in some businesses as long hair in others. A scruffy appearance can usually be quite easily remedied.

*Manner/social qualities.* Again, think of the people he will be dealing with. The right approach can be developed, so training can help here.

*Human understanding or empathy.* This is the ability to understand the other person's point of view, even if you do not necessarily agree with it. This is an essential quality in managers and salesmen. Again, it can be developed with practice.

*Persuasiveness and articulation.* Again, these are essential qualities. They can be developed by training. Again, think of the people he will be dealing with. Provided he is articulate, the accent does not usually matter very much.

*Intelligence.* Psychologists still cannot agree about what intelligence is. Still, you should be able to distinguish at least three or even five levels of intelligence, from very bright to very dull. You may not want a genius. If the job is fairly routine the very bright individual will get bored.

*Initiative and independence.* Since the salesman has to work alone, initiative and independence of mind are required. On the other hand, "prima donnas" are not usually required for most sales jobs.

*Ambition.* You may not want people who are too ambitious. There have to be Indians as well as Chiefs, and if there are not sufficient prospects for advancement in your own company, the ambitious man will leave.

*Enthusiasm.* Essential in a salesman, but it is partly your responsibility to keep it alive. Remember, too, that someone who has just left a job in which he has been bullied about by some autocrat will be in a sorry state. After three months or so he can become a changed personality.

*Patience, judgement, and creativity (bright ideas).* Are all required.

*Integrity.* Integrity cannot be qualified. He either has it or not.

*Loyalty.* You have to earn this, not expect it as a right.

Generally speaking, whilst you may want all these qualities in a high degree, you can never hope to get them. Therefore, you have to extend your range of choice down the scale to the point from which abilities can be developed and training is likely to be effective.

### EXAMPLES OF JOB SPECIFICATIONS AND MAN PROFILES

#### Agricultural Fertilizers & Feeds Ltd.*

*Job Specifications and Man Profiles for Salesmen and Development Officers*

INTRODUCTION. A.F. & F. Ltd. are agricultural merchants. Their main interest is the manufacture and sale of compound fertilizers

*An imaginary name.

to farmers in Barsetshire and surrounding counties. Of slightly lesser importance is the manufacture and sale of animal feed-stuffs. Since grass seed is associated with fertilizer usage, A.F. & F. are also involved in a major way in the processing of grass seed mixtures.

A.F. & F. are also agents for the sale of uncompounded nitrogenous fertilizers, weed-killers, insecticides and animal health products, manufactured by several chemical companies.

The major part of compounded and uncompounded fertilizers is sold retail to the farmer, but a valuable proportion is sold to other merchants via wholesale representatives. The area of operations is divided into sales districts, each with one or more sales offices. Retail salesmen work in defined territories. In sales offices there is a staff to support the field team. The sales team includes specialists in various technical capacities.

Within a sales district, field staff and all sales office staff are members of a sales team led by a District Sales Manager.

A.F. & F. buy home-grown produce, particularly grain, also hay and straw. This influences sales to the farmer, beneficially and is also used in settling farmers' accounts.

## THE CUSTOMER IS THE FARMER

### Job Specification of the A.F. & F. Salesman

The A.F. & F. salesman is the most important link between the Company and farmer. He works in a defined territory under the supervision of a District Sales Manager to whom he is responsible for all aspects of his work.

OBJECTIVES.

1. To sell and to buy in a manner designed to give maximum profit to the Company; this governed by Company policy as interpreted by his D.S.M.

2. To sell so as to maintain and increase the market share of compound fertilizers, slag (lime);
   compound feedstuffs;

grass, cereal and root seeds;

factored uncompounded fertilizers;

crop protection and specified animal health products.

3. To take part in overall development to increase market for these products.

4. To buy farmers' home-grown produce, in particular grain, also hay and straw.

RESPONSIBILITIES.

A. *Targets*

He will co-operate with his D.S.M. in agreeing product targets for his territory.

B. *Product knowledge*

He will:

1. be able to advise farmers on correct usage of all products handled by the company;
2. have an understanding of manufacture, processing and packaging of company products;
3. be familiar with farming practice in his territory and in particular with modern and developing farming techniques.

To achieve the above, he will:

(a) read company literature on products;
(b) follow company publicity in farming press and elsewhere;
(c) make use of technical service;
(d) *listen* to leading farmer customers;
(e) attend local farmers' meetings;
(f) make full use of all visits organized for salesmen, or salesmen plus farmers, to various centres—and special farm demonstrations arranged by A.F. & F.;
(g) participate in company training programmes and courses.

C. *Territory planning*

He will:

1. Prepare and use a calling plan based on
   (a) farm potential;

    (b)  markets;

    (c)  roads;

    (d)  frequency of call—that is, number of times farmer requires to be visited to secure worthwhile business;

    (e)  farm record cards.

2.  Arrange calls so that maximum time is spent in "face to face" selling to farmer.

3.  Ensure that all farmers and specialist farmers are visited regularly in his prescribed territory, excluding horticulturists.

This includes:

    (a)  those farmers buying A.F. & F. fertilizer from merchants with a view to selling all other products;

    (b)  existing customers who do not take certain lines;

    (c)  non-customers.

## D. *Planning the sale*

Prior to every call he will:

1.  Know the product he is going to sell, or precise reason for call.

2.  Have for each call a prepared sales presentation—

    OPENING

    DISCUSSION GUIDE LINES

        Creating attention, interest, desire, leading to decision and action.

    CLOSE

    RE-ENTRY

3.  Consider the timing of calls in relation to markets and best time of day to achieve good results.

## E. *Commercial knowledge*

He will:

1.  Make sure he understands Company policy.

2. In selling and buying, aim at maximum realization for company, consistent with retaining customer's business.

3. Be conversant with list prices, terms of sale and special rebates for all commodities he sells.

4. Ensure the company gets reasonable time to execute delivery of orders.

5. Utilize selectively, Company contracting and advisory services to increase sales. These services are as follows:
   fertilizer, lime and slag spreading;
   chemical spraying;
   seed drilling;
   mobile seed dressing;
   advisory services;
   farm management and recording services.

6. Be familiar with the company's accountancy system.

7. Make use of and understand, statistics produced by the company in so far as they affect his territory and sales district as a whole.

8. Understand the duties of commercial assistants and all other personnel in the district office.

F. *Farm produce*
He will:

1. Be knowledgeable on production, harvesting and quality of all farm-grown produce which is handled by the company.

2. Be able to assess market value of farmers' produce.

3. Co-operate with his colleagues in moving farm produce from customer to customer.

G. *Money collection*
He will:

1. Satisfy himself that all potential customers are financially sound before accepting an order.

2. If in doubt about an existing account, advise his District Sales Manager immediately.

3. Collect all debts due the company. In this respect he will attempt to encourage the maximum number of customers to pay direct to the accountancy office.
4. Purchase farm produce to balance accounts.
5. Practice company cash/cheque lodgement and receipt procedures.

## H. *Customer relations*
He will:
1. Ensure he is selling to the correct person.
2. Attend to customer complaints promptly and amicably and settle fairly.
3. Cultivate friendly relations with people who may influence successful selling—farmer's family, farm managers, factors, grieves and secretaries.
4. Be expected to offer service to farmers outside normal working hours.
5. Be attentive to the farmer and in this respect he will make no promises which cannot be kept; having made a precise offer or promise he will ensure it is carried out by the company or himself.
6. Take selected farmers on prearranged visits to various centres to promote interest in the company, company products and farming techniques which lead to sales.

## J. *Routine responsibilities*
He will:
1. Submit expense sheets promptly and properly completed.
2. Ensure that car accounts are submitted promptly and that his car is kept in good running order.
3. Attend meetings as arranged by his District Sales Manager.
4. Co-operate with his colleagues in the specialist and advisory service in the selection of suitable farms for publicity or trial purposes.
5. Attend selected local shows.

COMMUNICATIONS. He will:

1. Report competitors' activities in his territory to his D.S.M.
2. Pass on ideas to his D.S.M. which may lead to improvement in company's organization and selling; also report the effect that new ideas, or products, are having on the market.
3. Be in direct contact with, and call on the services of, commercial assistant, debt controller, development officer, order reception personnel, sales specialists.
4. Write orders precisely, legibly and in the manner requested by the company.
5. Submit reports when called for by his D.S.M.
6. Inform sales office of changes in customer addresses.

AUTHORITY. Within the limits of maximum and minimum prices at which goods may be sold and bought, he has authority to decide the price level at which to secure the order or make a purchase and make such decisions on the spot.

COMPANY'S RESPONSIBILITY TO SALESMAN

1. The company will supply a copy of the Staff Handbook to which he will refer for major aspects of company responsibility to him in respect of salary, superannuation, leave, sickness and removal expenses.

2. The company will meet all legitimate out-of-pocket expenses incurred in carrying out his duties. This includes expenses for meals away from home, postages and necessary entertainment of customers.

3. The company will provide a car.

4. The company will provide a telephone in the salesman's home, paying rental and telephone charges involved with company business.

5. The salesman may communicate on personal matters with the personnel department.

6. The company will provide continual training facilities.

TABLE 5.4. Man Profile of the A.F. & F. Salesman

**Statement of the Job to be done**

Under the direction of a District Sales Manager, the A.F. & F. salesman will sell A.F. & F. compound fertilizers, compound feedingstuffs, grass, root and cereal seeds, uncompounded fertilizer, crop protection and animal health products to the farmer and develop these markets. He will also buy from the farmer certain farm produce (particularly grain) on a reciprocal trading basis.

| Qualifications | Ideal | Variance profile | | Personal qualities (to be scored 0–5; scores of 3 and over are acceptable and must be so in first six. Scores of 2 and under are unacceptable) |
|---|---|---|---|---|
| 1. Age | 26 | 22 | 45 | 1. Good appearance |
| 2. Education | N.D.A. or S.D.A. | B.Sc.(Agric.) | Three 'O' Levels including English and mathematics | 2. Pleasing personality |
| | | | | 3. Confident manner |
| 3. Experience | Successful selling experience to farmers | Successful selling experience | Past association with farming or ancillary industry | 4. Self-expression |
| | | | | 5. Sincerity |
| | | | | 6. Enthusiasm |
| 4. Mobility | National | National | Local | 7. Persuasiveness |
| 5. Health record | No record of incapacitating illness | No record of incapacitating illness for 5 years | No record of incapacitating illness for 2 years | 8. Trustworthiness |
| | | | | 9. Initiative |
| 6. Driving licence | Clean | Clean | Minor offences only | 10. Ambition |
| 7. Marital status | Male—married with young family | Male—married | Male—single | 11. Sense of humour |
| | | | | 12. Sobriety |

*Job Specification of the A.F. & F. Development Officer*

The Development Officer is a technically qualified member of the sales team. He is executively responsible to the District Sales Manager and responsible to the Chief Technical Officer for the technical content of his work only.

OBJECTIVES

1. To increase the demand for A.F. & F. compound fertilizers and uncompounded fertilizers.

2. To create a demand for new products to the A.F. & F. selling range in respect of fertilizers, feedstuffs, crop protection products and farm seeds.

3. To increase and service the A.F. & F. share of existing markets for fertilizers, slag, feedstuffs, crop protection products and farm seeds.

RESPONSIBILITIES

A. *Product and commercial knowledge*

He will:
1. be fully conversant with company products;
2. have thorough understanding of farming systems in his district and also of wider aspects of British agriculture.
3. Ensure that he
   (a) has a knowledge of selling techniques,
   (b) participates in sales training,
   (c) associates himself with sales objectives and targets in his district.
   (d) plans calls to give maximum "face to face" time with farmer.

B. *The salesman*

The work of the Development Officer is initiated through the retail salesman. First-class relations with the salesman are essential.

He will:

1. On salesman's request, provide technical information so that this can be passed to farmer.

2. Improve salesmen's product knowledge.

3. Help junior salesmen to improve their product knowledge.

4. Assist salesmen during special product selling campaigns.

5. Assist salesmen with customer complaints.

C. *The farmer as an individual*

He will:

1. Encourage the use of modern management techniques in crop, grass and animal husbandry (cattle and sheep) leading to increased usage of fertilizers.

2. Concentrate on milk production in Barsetshire and beef and cereal production in Hamptonshire.
   To assist him he will use:
   (a) soil sampling and silage sampling;
   (b) cropping and fertilizer programmes;
   (c) information from farm management and recording services—standards and gross margin costs.

3. Formulate cattle and sheep feeding programmes with a view to incorporating A.F. & F. compounds along with home-grown produce. To assist him he will use:
   (a) silage sampling;
   (b) A.F. & F. Dairy Food calculator.

4. Attend to customer complaints, calling in the services of other specialists where necessary.

5. Use A.F. & F. services which have a bearing on advice he is giving a particular customer, e.g. fertilizer, lime and slag spreading, and cereal seed dressing.

6. Keep up to date on building and machinery developments to help him advise farmers on farming and stock management policy.

D. *The farmer as a group*

He will:

1.  Arrange and participate in the following:
    (a) farm walks and demonstrations with a view to achieving objectives stated;
    (b) visits to A.F. & F. sites where the object is selling specific products or management techniques;
    (c) Public meetings for the farming community.
2.  Create opportunities to speak on aspects of his work.
3.  Create opportunities to write articles with Company's approval of content.

E. *The company*

He will:

1.  Select sites for product trials.
2.  Co-operate with the Publicity Department by procuring photographs for inclusion in A.F. & F. literature.
3.  On D.S.M.'s instructions, help to assess individual farmers' profitability.
4.  Be present at local shows.
5.  Attend area sales meetings as instructed by his D.S.M. and meetings organized by the Chief Technical Officer.
6.  Attend to complaints which require investigation and report on appropriate form the position to his D.S.M.

COMMUNICATIONS

He will:

1.  (a) With all letters to farmers ensure that a copy is sent to the salesman and his D.S.M.
    (b) Ensure that copies of soil sampling reports, cropping and feeding programmes are sent to the salesmen.
    (c) Where no letter or report is necessary, ensure that salesmen are informed of visits he has made to their farmers and reasons for them.

2. Advise his D.S.M. and the Chief Technical Officer of competitors' activities and developments in his area.
3. Report important trends in agricultural practices for his area, especially where they will affect sales of company products in the future, and anticipate the demand for new products.
4. Ensure D.S.M. is advised promptly of any matter of a technical nature concerning the running of the district.
5. Prepare monthly a report covering the main areas of his work, especially those of interest to the company. This will be circulated to the Chief Technical Officer, D.S.M.'s and salesmen in his area.
6. Compile lists of college personnel, bankers, members of the D.A.F.S. and vets in his area. From these he will circulate information which may improve relations with these groups. He will know the key men in the above services.
7. Communicate with product managers on technical matters.
8. Liaise closely with the Farm Management Adviser/ Recorder in his area.

AUTHORITY. He has full authority to speak to the individual customer or collectively to farming audiences on any technical subject, giving the Company's viewpoint.

COMPANY RESPONSIBILITIES TO DEVELOPMENT OFFICER

1. The company will supply a copy of the Staff Handbook to which he will refer for major aspects of company responsibility to him in respect of salary, superannuation, leave, sickness and removal expenses.

2. The company will meet all legitimate out-of-pocket expenses incurred in carrying out his duties. This includes expenses for meals away from home, postages and necessary entertainment of customers.

TABLE 5.5. Man Profile of the A.F. & F. Development Officer

### Statement of the Job to be done

Under the supervision of a District Sales Manager, the A.F. & F. Development Officer will create and increase the demand for A.F. & F. compound fertilizers, compound feedingstuffs, grass, root and cereal seeds, straight nitrogen, crop protection and animal health products. He will also carry out trials and demonstrations as instructed by the chief Technical Officer.

| Qualifications | Ideal | Variance profile | | Personal qualities (to be scored 0–5; scores of 3 and over are acceptable and must be so in first six. Scores of 2 and under are unacceptable) |
|---|---|---|---|---|
| 1. Age | 28 | 23 | 35 | 1. Good appearance |
| 2. Education | B.Sc.(Agric.) | B.Sc.(Agric.)Hons. | B.Sc.(Agric.) | 2. Pleasing personality |
| 3. Experience | Post-graduate experience of field selling in agriculture | Graduate with special abilities or farming background | Practical experience of agriculture or official advisory services | 3. Confident manner |
| | | | | 4. Self-expression |
| | | | | 5. Sincerity |
| 4. Mobility | National | National | National | 6. Enthusiasm |
| 5. Health record | No record of incapacitating illness | No record of incapacitating illness for 5 years | No record of incapacitating illness for 2 years | 7. Persuasiveness |
| | | | | 8. Trustworthiness |
| 6. Driving licence | Clean | Clean | Minor offences only | 9. Initiative |
| 7. Marital status | Male—married with young family | Male—married | Male—single | 10. Ambition |
| | | | | 11. Sense of humour |
| | | | | 12. Sobriety |

3. The company will provide a car.

4. The company will provide a telephone in his home, paying rental and telephone charges involved with company business.

5. He may communicate on personal matters with the Personnel Department.

6. He will be given opportunity to travel and attend courses to improve his agricultural knowledge.

# CHAPTER 6

# IMPLEMENTATION

## RECRUITING

YOU cannot start recruiting until you have a proper specification of the job to be performed and a clear idea of the qualifications and personal qualities required of the man to do the job.

There are three main approaches to recruitment:

personal solicitation,

public advertising,

specialist employment agencies/selection consultants,

and a variety of sources:

own non-sales staff,

introductions through your own staff,

customer's recommendations,

competitors,

salesmen in other trades,

schools, universities, etc.,

and, again, specialist employment agencies.

### Approaches

It is equally essential, whichever approach you use, to have a job specification and man profile.

If you are personally going to invite someone who has a good reputation or has attracted your attention in some other way, and whom you have known for some time, to join your staff, make absolutely certain that he conforms to your man profile. This method of recruitment is probably the best, because you will have had an opportunity to see how the man performs before you make your proposal. On the other hand, you may have grown to like him personally as an individual and this could affect the objectivity of your judgement.

If you are going to advertise publicly, in whatever medium, the press or your own company notice board, you are selling your vacancy in competition with numerous other would-be employers. In today's conditions of high employment, most candidates have a considerable choice of job or company. Therefore, whilst a candidate will have to sell himself to you, you have to sell him:

the opportunity in a selling career for personal achievement;

the particular benefits and advantages of a selling job in your company;

the idea that serving the company's customers is a great responsibility entrusted to him—he will be responsible for its most valuable assets.

Therefore, your advertisement should be designed and placed to have at least as much selling power as your general advertising. It is only in this way that you can attract the most suitable applicants. Your company's advertising agency, or one of the specialists in personnel advertising will be pleased to help you.

The advertisement should include:

---

## AN ATTENTION-GETTING HEADLINE

**The Company**
a brief, but interesting, statement about the company's business

**The Job**
a brief statement of the Job Specification

**The Man**
a brief statement of the Man Profile

**The Reward**
the salary, perks and prospects

Please apply in writing, with details of your career to date, to:
Your name
Sales Director/Manager
Your Company's name and address

---

FIG. 6.1

It is most important that your advertisement should be in the form shown in Fig. 6.1 because it starts the selection procedure for you. Generally speaking, people are reasonably honest with themselves, and so you will get applications, apart from a few cranks, of course, from people who believe that they have the ability to do the job and would enjoy doing it. Another point is that it tells likely applicants that you have planned the job to be done carefully and know what sort of man you are looking for.

Check through today's papers and see how many advertisements are laid out like this—very few indeed. Most of the display advertisements could hardly be called informative, and just about all those—the "death creates a vacancy, please apply to box XYZ" type—in the classified columns, are unlikely to attract the slightest attention.

An important point about the financial reward; make this figure explicit—not something vague like "salary according to age and qualifications". Furthermore, instead of putting "between $£x$–$£y$", put "about $£z$". Applicants generally have good reason to doubt the integrity and good intentions of would-be employers, so they will suspect that you only intend to offer the lower figure, $£x$, and have put in the higher figure, $£y$, as bait.

Finally, ask them to write to you personally, not to some nameless functionary.

Specialist employment agencies or selection consultants can be a great help. They can take a lot of the hard work out of recruiting and selecting for a fee, usually 15% of the salary, for the position to be filled.

They can help you draw up the job specification and man profile. They may have suitable people on their books already. They can prepare and place the advertisement for you. They can prepare a short list of suitable candidates for your final selection. You should use them if you must remain anonymous.

**Sources**

Many companies like to promote from within, and, whether this is your company's policy or not, there are probably some promising young men in your internal staff who would like an opportunity to join the sales force. This may or may not be an advantage. You will not need to spend as much time teaching them about the company's policies and procedures as you would external recruits. On the other hand, internal staff may not have the independence of mind that is required of salesmen, and too much "in-breeding" is undesirable.

You can use your own staff as talent spotters. If you do this, make it clear to them that anyone they recommend will have to take his chance along with any other candidates, so that they will not feel aggrieved if you have to reject their nominees.

A customer will usually be willing to recommend a good salesman, particularly if he knows that he is unhappy working with his present employers.

It is difficult to make any general statement about recruiting staff from competitors, customers or suppliers, or "poaching" as it is called. Practices vary greatly from industry to industry, and company to company. In some cases it is considered highly unethical, and in others perfectly legitimate. Contracts of employment may be taken seriously by both employer and employee, or not, as the case may be.

In certain industries there are "gentlemen's agreements" not to poach each other's staff. Such agreements usually work against the interests of the individual. If he wishes to leave an employer for some reason or another on his own initiative, he is unlikely to be offered a job by a competitor, unless he is a particularly valuable prize, within the same industry. Although the law exists to safeguard the rights of the individual, in this instance, no law can compel a firm to take on a competitor's ex-employee if they do not wish to.

So, if you wish to recruit a particularly good man from any of these sources, consider the "goodwill" aspect first. Is it considered ethical or not in your own company or in the industry, trade or profession generally? Even if it is thought to be ethical, there may be some legal difficulties, so you will probably have to consult your legal advisers.

Salesmen from other trades, you will usually recruit by advertising.

Some of the larger companies have special recruiting campaigns in schools and universities. Even if your company does not go to this length in recruiting, you should keep in touch with careers masters/advisers in local schools and colleges.

Finally, you should budget for your requirements in advance, and if possible have a waiting list of suitable candidates.

## SELECTING

### Preselection

If your advertisement has been drawn-up and placed in the manner described, and the rewards have been pitched at the right level, it will by itself start the selection procedure for you.

Since conditions in the employment market are continually changing, there can be no general rule about the number of replies you can expect. If you get hundreds or just two or three, though, you can be sure your advertisement was wrong.

When you have received the letters of application, compare each one with your man profile.

Reject all those who clearly do not match the man profile either way—both those who exceed your requirements and those who do not reach them. If you get a high proportion of unsuitable applicants, you can be sure, again, that your advertisement was wrong. Do not be tempted to take on people who are much too good for the job, because they will quickly get bored and frustrated, and leave you at the earliest opportunity. On the other hand, the dangers of accepting the best of a bad lot are equally obvious.

If you are quite satisfied that the job specification and man profile are correct, and it appears that it is the level of reward that is attracting the wrong type, you should re-advertise at a different level. If the level required to attract suitable applicants is higher than you are currently paying your salesmen, you may have to review the whole salary structure.

To the ones you are rejecting, write polite letters of regret, saying that on reading their applications it does not appear that their qualifications are in line with the job you have to offer. Thank them for their interest. This is only a matter of simple courtesy, but many companies neglect this point.

To all those who appear suitable, send a fuller version of the advertisement, that is, a statement about the company's business, and the complete job specification and man profile; and a standard application form.

This again does some of the selection for you. It will impress those who are really interested in the job. Those who are not will opt out by themselves. The application form will enable you to get all the information you require in a coherent form.

If you are designing an application form there are several points you should observe. The first is to ensure that your questions are strictly relevant. Secondly, you should allow adequate space for the answers. This seems simply a matter of common sense, but these two points are frequently neglected. The third point is concerned with the question about the applicant's salary history. Remember, if you offer him a job, it should be at your valuation, not someone else's; and some people may inflate the figures they give anyway.

When you have checked all the completed application forms, again, reject all those who appear unsuitable. If each step in the process has been carried out correctly up to this point, you should, in fact, have few rejects.

You now have your first short list. Ask these men to come for an interview.

### Interviewing

The purpose of an interview is to establish the facts about the candidate and to find out whether there is a coherent pattern in his behaviour.

You should resist any temptation to evaluate the information as it is being elicited. The assessment of the candidate's suitability should be made after the interview has been completed.

The recommended procedure for interviewing executive or sales staff is a series, preferably three, of man to man confrontations in a businesslike but relaxed atmosphere. It is only in this way that you can encourage the candidate to full expression.

Other techniques of interviewing have been devised.

The group method, where a dozen candidates are observed discussing a selected topic by, say, three selectors is the one to use if you are looking for bland committeemen.

The board-type interview, with up to a dozen selectors interviewing a single candidate, is very difficult to co-ordinate. For this reason it is likely to serve little purpose at all, unless you want to see how good the candidate is at fielding unrelated and irrelevant questions. There is a danger that the candidate may take the initiative, because from his point of view, it resembles a public meeting and he has an audience to address.

The police and security services have devised a variety of techniques for the purpose of interrogating suspected criminals and spies. Some companies and individual selection consultants have attempted to adapt these techniques to their own purposes. This is quite unforgivable. They may be admirable for the purpose for which they were devised, but for the purpose of staff selection they are quite ineffective. Their use for this purpose is, at best, just silly; at worst it can be macabre and even tragic.

There are three essentials for conducting a man to man interview.

*Preparation:*

   study your man profile;

   study all known facts about the applicant;

   note gaps in information, particularly previous employment record;

   decide what information you are prepared to give—how much and in what detail;

   and make notes.

*Peace:*

relaxed atmosphere; easy chairs face to face, not across a large
 desk, cigarettes, tea, coffee, etc.;
set the applicant at ease;
meet as equals, not as superior and inferior;
no interruptions.

*Patience:*

check the man profile;
lead the applicant who is diffident;
head off the applicant who talks too much;
never score off the applicant;
keep control of yourself and the interview.

Remember that the candidate is a stranger wearing a mask.
He is probably a bit nervous and apprehensive, so you must
establish good rapport. Let the candidate do approximately
75% of the talking—you just ask questions and prompt him.
Start off by asking about his journey. He will usually respond to
this, and the answer could be important. Then ask him about his
present job. This is a subject he should be able to talk about
knowledgeably—his company, their products and markets, etc.
Listen attentively and ask pertinent questions to show that you
are interested and understand what he is talking about. On the
other hand, do not let him ramble on and on. As this part of the
interview proceeds the two of you will become better acquainted
with each other and establish rapport. Sometimes it may be
desirable to adopt a sympathetic "bedside-manner" in the early
stages of the interview, particularly if, for genuine reasons, he is
desperately unhappy in his present job.

Having established rapport, you can then proceed to probe
for all the other information required which you have previously
noted down. Remember that you are more likely to get the
information you require by polite enquiry, rather than overbearing
interrogation. Never ask him to try to sell you something. This

is quite inappropriate in a selection interview. Remember also that he is weighing you up as a prospective boss.

Timing is important. Spread interviews sufficiently to ensure adequate time, and arrange appointments so that no two applicants are likely to meet each other.

Finally, assess the candidate's suitability on the basis of all the information together when the interview has been completed.

This interview should be followed by another similar one conducted by a colleague. Provided that there has been agreement beforehand, on the details of man profile, a second opinion on the candidate's suitability will help minimize the chances of a serious mistake in selection. After this screening, you will require yet another meeting, of a less formal nature, to confirm the assessment and make an offer of employment to the candidate.

One final word of warning. Psychological techniques attempting to measure intelligence, personality, attitudes and aptitudes objectively, may be used to complement, *and only to complement*, the foregoing procedure. Their value has by no means been proved conclusively, and they can be extremely dangerous in unqualified hands.

Again, this selection process is laborious and time consuming. It is not infallible, but it will help you to reduce greatly the likelihood of making a mistake. Remember how expensive a salesman is.

If you have your own personnel department or employ selection consultants to do the initial screening, remember that the person who is actually going to be responsible for the man must make the final decision. He cannot then, at a later stage, if anything goes wrong, complain that the man was imposed upon him.

### TRAINING

Training is inevitable. It is expensive too, but lack of training is even more expensive. The days when you could hire a salesman, give him a price list and some samples, and tell him to get on with it, never were.

## Objectives

The purpose of training is to change people. The changes desired may be in the degree of factual knowledge possessed, the understanding of concepts, the level of intellectual and physical skills and in values and attitudes. Some of these changes may be achieved in a very short time, others may take months or years to achieve. They may require continual reinforcement having once been achieved. Therefore training must be a continuous process.

In any course of training, the objectives or changes desired must be established. Each case will be unique. In the absence of objectives any training will do. Much training is wasted because the changes to be achieved are never specified. Professional educators and trainers tend to get carried away by the sophistication and subtleties of technique. Provided that the purposes have been established, the crudest techniques of instruction can be very effective. If you do not know what you wish to achieve, any technique will be equally ineffective.

Furthermore, the objectives of any course of training must be communicated to, and understood by, those undergoing it. They must be sold the idea. They must believe that it is worthwhile and actively participate in the process.

Again, if this is not done, any training is likely to be a waste of time. If you are just starting a formal training function within your company, the task of selling the idea will be doubly difficult. There will be the usual resistance to change—"we've got on very well without training so far, so why do we need it now?" Those who believe that they have hitherto been doing a good job will resent the implication that they have not. The "know-alls" will prefer to remain ignorant.

The way to overcome these difficulties, particularly with the older men, is to invite their active co-operation and participation. You can point out that with their years of experience, they have an invaluable contribution to make. On no account must it appear that it is being imposed on them.

In general, a successful salesman, and a successful manager for that matter too, is distinguished by:

- (i) his depth of knowledge and understanding of people and things;
- (ii) the ability to use this knowledge to achieve profitable results for himself and the company he serves.

In general, therefore, the objectives of any course of sales training are:

1. To increase the salesmen's knowledge and understanding of:
   - (i) the company: its operations, policies and procedures;
   - (ii) the company's product(s)/service(s), their values and the markets for them;
   - (iii) the company's competitors and their operations, product(s)/service(s), etc.;
   - (iv) the principles, methods and psychology of selling.
2. To improve the salesmen's ability to apply this knowledge to achieve better results.

The starting-point for establishing the objectives in detail is to measure the difference between:

- (i) the actual performance in the job and the standards specified in the job specification;
- (ii) the actual qualifications and personal qualities of your salesmen and the ideals you have already specified in your man profile.

You will derive this information partly from your selection procedure and from the control procedures which we shall discuss in Chapter 7.

Training must be a continuous process. Clearly, though, the requirements of new recruits—initial training—will differ considerably from that required by experienced salesmen—stimulation or reinforcement training.

Your training programme should be drawn up to include all the elements of the salesmen's job outlined earlier. You will be able to formulate your ideas about the quantity and quality of training required for individual salesmen and the sales force as a whole, by considering the actual levels of knowledge and ability compared with the desired standards for each element.

## Methods

A wide variety of methods are available. Remember that the simplest techniques are usually perfectly adequate and do not get carried away by fascinating pieces of hardware.

(i) *Lectures*. Plan lectures around a few key points. Do not attempt to cover too much ground in one talk.

(ii) *Visual aids* may be used to good effect. These should, however, only be shown while the relevant subject matter is under discussion. An ordinary blackboard may be perfectly adequate. "Flip" charts are very useful. Slides can be used. Overhead projectors with lots of gadgets on them distract attention. They usually get in the way of both the lecturer and the screen. Films should not just be shown to get over the difficult hour after lunch. They are very good for illustrating the principles of selling in general terms, but many salesmen have difficulty in relating the generalizations to their own particular problems. The best way to show them is to introduce them very carefully first; then show them; rewind; and then show again; stopping after each episode for discussion.

(iii) *Programmed instruction*. This can be in a variety of forms; either as programmed texts in book form, or in roll form for putting on a "teaching machine"; or as tape recorded lessons used in conjunction with texts. The main advantages of this kind of instruction are that: it is self-pacing, the student learns at his own pace, not that of a class which may wish to go faster or slower; the information is given in small amounts for easy assimilation; and it demands the student's active participation.

The trouble is, though, that whilst there is a bewildering array of hardware available, there are not enough people trained and qualified to write the programmed texts. Although texts on general topics are available, you would almost certainly require special "tailor-made" ones for your own purposes.

(iv) *Discussion groups* are very valuable indeed because they encourage participation and cross fertilization of ideas. Again, they can be preceded by films, sketches or illustrations. Syndicates can be formed to study, analyse and report on the application of selected sales principles, the presentation of material, and the handling of specified sales situations.

(v) *Simulated sales situations*, conducted in small groups using audio or video-tape equipment are very effective provided that the barrier of self-consciousness has been carefully eliminated. Your own company buyer will be delighted to participate, so that he can present his point of view.

(vi) *Instruction and demonstration in the field* is potentially the most effective method of all provided that:

there has been a sound analysis of the particular sales situation beforehand; selling principles and techniques have also been examined and are clearly understood, so that in the field their application can be related to:

(a) the type of selling,
(b) the type of customer,
(c) the type of product/service,
(d) the purpose of the particular interview,

and constructive criticism of performance is combined with practical demonstration, whenever this is possible.

## DIRECTION

Direction of the individual salesmen and the co-ordination of the sales force as a whole is achieved by the specification of the jobs to be performed.

Again, we can see how vitally important these job specifications are.

Direction is not achieved simply by imposing the job specification upon the individual salesman. He must understand that it has not been drawn up arbitrarily, but that it is based upon the best available factual information. He must understand how the territory has been planned and he must agree that the quantitative sales targets are achievable and the work loads reasonable and within his capacity. Again, as with the need for training, you have to sell the job to him.

## MOTIVATION

Motivation is the will to achieve results. There has been much study, and much speculation, and a great deal written about what makes a man work. Sometimes motivation, or "man management" is mistaken for the totality of management. It is not. Before you can motivate a person, the results desired must be specified. The process of motivation starts when the desired results, objectives, targets or goals to be achieved by the individual are clearly communicated to him. Motivation cannot exist without a purpose; only children can get excited about nothing.

Therefore, the agreed job specification is the start of the process of motivation.

Some, a very few, salesmen will need no further incentive to achieve results beyond this. They are natural self-starters; to them selling is the most fascinating job in the world. The majority of salesmen will, however, require special stimulation and encouragement, and even the best will require sympathetic help from time to time.

Selling is a difficult job. There are frequent disappointments and many frustrations. It is a lonely life. The salesman spends a lot of time away from home and although he spends much of it with other people, there is little real human contact. His hours are irregular.

Since the customer is omnipotent, the salesman is in an inferior position. Society as a whole mistakenly tends to regard him as inferior too.

On top of all this he has the usual personal problems that beset anyone else.

His job becomes virtually impossible if, in addition, his sales manager is uncomprehending and unsympathetic towards his problems.

Perhaps the best approach in motivating your salesmen is to treat them in the same manner that you expect them to treat their important customers, and in the manner in which you wish your superiors would treat you. Remember, example comes from the top.

In addition to communicating the desired results to be achieved clearly, you should:

give him all the information he requires to do the job;

inform him of his progress towards his objectives;

build on his strengths, and minimize the effects of his weaknesses, by training.

## Problems of Remuneration

"It's only monkeys that work for peanuts" is an old and true saying. However, it is equally true that money is not everything. Money, by itself, will only work as an effective incentive in the case of people close to or on the level of bare subsistence.

Above this level, the other human factors of motivation become increasingly important. As indicated above, the salesman's job is a difficult one, and thus he needs an especially considerate, sympathetic and supportive style of leadership from his sales manager. On the other hand, difficult though it is, the job can also be an extremely satisfying one in itself.

Thus, provided that the salesman receives the right kind of leadership and the job itself is interesting and satisfying the financial reward is only one factor—and an important one to be sure—in motivation. To put this the other way round, if the right kind of leadership is lacking and the job is not satisfying, then money by itself will not motivate a salesman to achieve results.

However, since the subject of remuneration is dear to us all, let us consider the various methods of payment of salesmen—about which there is so much argument.

There are three principal methods:

    (i)   commission only,
    (ii)  basic salary plus commission,
    (iii) salary only.

In considering the remuneration of salesmen we have to go back approximately 3000 years in history. The very earliest kind of salesman was what could be described as a "merchant salesman" who not only bought and sold goods, but also financed, warehoused and shipped them. He was an independent businessman, and as such made an entrepreneurial profit or loss. Merchants of this kind still exist today of course.

As communications improved and trade expanded, even in the earliest days, these general merchants started to specialize in certain activities. Some became bankers, others became shippers and yet others became "broker-salesmen" selling on "consignment" or commission. It is important to remember this, because it is only within recent times that a money economy has become general. From the very earliest times, when the majority of the population were either paid in kind or, as slaves, not paid at all, salesmen have always been paid in money.

During the Industrial Revolution the independent travelling broker-salesman representing several manufacturers was an important and respected member of the business community. Towards the end of the last century manufacturers started to employ their own full-time salesmen. Since it was the traditional method of remuneration, these full-time employees were paid a commission on the sales they made.

The commission-only system of payment is still used of course, but it has many serious disadvantages for both employer and employee alike. Since the salesman is virtually an independent entrepreneur, the employer has little control over his activities. He cannot be effectively directed. Generally speaking commission-only salesmen are either very good indeed or utterly useless.

The main advantages to the employer are that selling costs are completely variable; that is, the cost of sales is directly related to sales volume. There are no overheads. The salesman has a straightforward financial incentive to produce results.

So far as the salesman is concerned, he has the advantage of being his own boss. On the other hand he has little security. There are no perks. Also the rewards are not usually directly related to effort; some territories may be very rich and others poor. Even if the territories have equal potentials, the work loads are likely to be different.

The commission-only system is little used these days as a method of payment for full-time employed salesmen. It is, however, still used extensively for independent or freelance agents, distributors or brokers.

In the early part of this century Charles Bedaux set up in business as a consultant in production engineering, initially in the U.S.A., then in Great Britain, and later in France. Although work study had been developed by Frederick Taylor, Bedaux was the first to sell the idea successfully to industrialists generally.

Work study is concerned with the examination and improvement of methods, and with the measurement of work content in order to establish standards of performance. This information can then be used to plan and control the utilization of labour, and of financial and productive resources. The more routine and repetitive the work, the easier it is to establish accurate standards of work content. In cases where the work is not routine and the content is difficult to measure, such as in maintenance engineering or in selling operations, crude standards of performance, which are quite adequate for planning and control purposes, can be established.

Bedaux found, however, that once having installed his system in a client's factory, it had to be firmly "locked in". This was because the standards of supervision were generally poor and clients soon tired of the necessary associated system of documentation and complained of too much paper work. Of course, if the reporting system was neglected, the clients were no better off than before. So, to "lock in" the system Bedaux also installed a financial incentive scheme, which consisted of a guaranteed basic wage and pro-rata bonus payments according to performance above a certain level. This is a two-edged weapon. On the one hand, it is an incentive for the operatives to work harder. On the other hand, and this is much more important, it forces the management to keep the system going. As indicated earlier, simply telling the operative what is expected of him and how he is performing, and instructing him in the right methods, is incentive enough. Incompetent management, however, has to be made to do this by the threat of having an uproar on the factory floor if they discontinue the bonus payments. Bedaux pointed out that the bonus is really a payment to the operative for managing himself in the absence of good supervision. This is, of course, not generally known or even acknowledged. So financial incentive schemes became all the rage in industry, and people have tried to apply them to every sphere of activity. Sometimes they have been completely ineffective because management had not defined the goals or targets and the means to be adopted in achieving them. Sometimes they have had disastrous results because either the work content could not be measured accurately or the wrong targets were specified. Ideally, they should only be applied in cases where the work content can be measured accurately; that is, in routine and repetitive operations.

It is not possible to establish 100% accurate workloads or sales targets in selling operations. They can, at best, only be good estimates. Whilst they are quite adequate for planning and controlling the activities of the sales force, they are not sufficiently accurate to form the basis of an incentive payment scheme. If no attempt has been made to establish work loads and sales targets, or the estimates are very rough indeed, an incentive scheme will serve little purpose at all.

Nevertheless, a vast number of incentive payment schemes have been invented to spur on salesmen to achieve results. In many cases the desired results have not been specified. Where targets have been established they have occasionally been either hopelessly inaccurate or incorrectly specified. Whether targets have been set or not, the bonus or commission is usually paid as a percentage of the gross sales revenue. It should be remembered that maximizing sales volume is not the same as maximizing contribution to overhead and profit.* Directing salesmen to maximize sales volume can be extremely dangerous. They will concentrate on those products which, although easy to sell, may not be very profitable.

Such schemes vary from the comparatively simple—either a low basic salary and high commission or high basic salary and low commission, paid on sales turnover, to extremely complicated rating systems. The latter are usually very expensive to administer. Even if the salesmen understand how they work, the wages and salaries department may not. Numerous mistakes are likely to be made, which cause endless argument and much bad feeling between the sales and financial departments.

Since the majority of salesmen are paid on the basis of a basic salary plus a variable bonus or commission of some sort, what has been said above may shatter some cherished illusions. Whilst these are the author's own opinions, they have been confirmed by his colleague and editor of this series, Douglas Smallbone, in an extensive research project covering 450 companies.

The last system of payment is that of a straightforward salary. Because there is no financial incentive, motivation to achieve results must be provided in the way outlined earlier, that is, by good management. Good management can provide the necessary motivation by itself. An additional financial inducement to reward the salesman for managing himself is only necessary in the absence of good sales management. Furthermore, the salary-only system is simple to administer, it is easy to understand, it is fair, and it enables the sales manager to direct the total selling effort—that is, all those activities necessary to achieve optimum profitability, not just those which achieve immediate maximum sales volume in the short term.

Again, this is not just the dogmatic opinion of the author. More and more companies are coming to the same conclusion.

*See Chapter 9 on Pricing.

Having said all that, there are other peripheral techniques of motivation which may be either permanent features, such as pension schemes and other perquisites, or which provide occasional reinforcing stimuli. In the latter category are such items as competitions, special bonuses and awards, weekend "conferences" at some pleasant resort, and ladies' nights—as a token of appreciation of their support.

CHAPTER 7

# CONTROL

**INTRODUCTION**

IN THIS system of management the process of control is that objectives, goals, targets or standards are established;

> the variance between the actual performance achieved and that desired is measured impartially and as objectively as possible;
> action is taken to ensure that future performance conforms to the desired standard.

The key word is "action". Control must be dynamic, and this process must be continuous and carried out in every sphere of activity of the company—not least in the activities of the sales force.

The control systems available to a business enterprise or any other organization are essentially crude. The control systems found in nature—the human body for instance—are inconceivably elegant and complex. Even if we ever achieve a complete understanding of how they work, we shall probably never be able to duplicate them.

Many of the systems we have invented for controlling mechanical, electromechanical and electronic devices are highly sophisticated. Many writers and philosophers of management have tried to draw parallels between the control of such devices and the control of organizations. Although their studies have produced many valuable insights, they have also produced some very unfortunate, and even disastrous, results. People and organizations are not machines, and the real or apparent similarities must not be stretched too far.

The "organomechanical" approach—to coin a phrase—certainly works well in the navigation of a ship for instance. The desired goal—port in this case—is specified. In deciding upon the appropriate means—the route—the charts and tide tables are consulted, the capabilities of the crew and engines are known, but the weather remains more or less unpredictable. Having established the route, progress towards the destination can be measured by fixing the ship's position at regular intervals. If the ship is found to be off course, corrective action can be taken by the helmsman and/or the engineers to bring it back on to course. Instruments such as charts, tidal predictions, weather forecasts, compasses, sextants, depth sounders, radar, radio direction finders and automatic pilots are available as *aids* to navigation. Navigation is an art, although it makes much use of science. No matter how sophisticated his instruments, the navigator has ultimately to rely on his own judgement, make the decisions, give the appropriate orders and see that they are carried out, himself. The navigator who relies entirely on his instruments to do the navigation for him is asking for trouble and usually gets it.

This approach is practiced in its most extreme form in repetitive engineering or assembly work—such as in the motor industry. The production targets can be set and results measured very accurately indeed, and thus very tight control over the manufacturing process can be achieved. The pace is set by the machine and the man has to accommodate to it.

Whilst the results in terms of physical output may be very great, the effects on the human cogs in the machine are anything but benign. As we are only too well aware, the manager who relies on his machines to manage for him gets all the strikes and labour troubles he deserves.

When it comes to evaluating the effects of the various media we are using to communicate with the market, we are faced with a problem which is entirely different in character and magnitude to that of, say, measuring the output of a machine shop.

For one thing, although the process of communication is predictable to a certain extent, it is certainly anything but mechanical. Also we would like to be able to measure the individual effects of all the media in the mixture—that is, the product or service itself, the price, the sales force, the advertising, sales promotion and public relations activities and the physical distribution system—acting in concert against the economy and indirect competition in general, and direct competition in particular. The yardstick we use to judge the total effect is, of course, the sales volume. However, it is virtually impossible to evaluate precisely the part played by one particular medium, say the sales force, in producing this combined result. We know, for instance, that if the product is exceptionally good it will still sell itself even if everything else is wrong. If the product is wrong, then no amount of sales pressure and promotion will sell it. When the product is similar to its competitors in quality and price, then the critical factor may be either wider distribution and better availability, a superior sales force, better advertising, better packaging or better service.

To use a musical analogy, it is rather like conducting an orchestra. The parts written for individual instruments would sound very odd played by themselves, but in combination they produce a symphony. To take this analogy a step further, we could have a brass band and an organ both playing different tunes in other parts of the hall—to represent the competition, and a fog-horn blasting-off intermittently—to represent the economy. The combined effect of this is left to your imagination.

This analogy is very apt in fact. Just as it is the composer's art to visualize the combined effect of all the instruments playing together, so it is the marketing man's art to visualize the combined effect of the various media working in concert against the economy and competition.

At the present stage of development the visualization of the combined effect of media is still very much of an art. Although serious attempts are being made to make it more scientific, it will probably forever remain more an art than a science. There will still be room for the genius.

It may seem then that it is rather a futile exercise to try to evaluate the performance of an individual medium. This is not so. First of all it is possible to establish targets that are agreed to be reasonable; then by investigation of the customer interface, to decide what media are required—even if not the proportions. Initially, a rough approximation to the right proportions can be gauged by reference to the competition and possibly other companies operating in different markets, but whose problems are basically similar. As indicated earlier, in planning the activities of the sales force, an arbitrary decision has to be made as to the appropriate call frequency. It is perfectly reasonable to make assumptions in the absence of factual evidence, provided that they are recognized for what they are and are continually questioned.

Having established that a sales force is an essential component of the media mixture, even if it is not possible to evaluate precisely the effect it has in producing the results in terms of sales volume by itself, it is possible to evaluate its performance in terms of the other yardsticks contained in the operating plans and job specifications you have already laid down.

The problem of determining the effect that advertising has in producing the final result is exactly the same. In many cases we are still no nearer to understanding its role than the first Lord Leverhulme, who said that he knew that half of his advertising expenditure was wasted, but he was not sure which half. Nevertheless, even if it is not possible to evaluate the effect of advertising in terms of sales volume by itself, it is possible to evaluate it in terms of other yardsticks such as:

| | |
|---|---|
| Message Registration | how much of the message sticks in the target audience's mind. |
| Brand Preference Levels | from "awareness" up through the scale to "first choice". |
| Product Image | how the target audience perceives the product. |

It is hardly surprising therefore that professional accountants, who can measure to the nearest halfpenny, or engineers who are used to dealing with microns, tend to be very sceptical about the validity of the marketing concept in general and all selling activities in particular.

## EVALUATION OF SALESMEN'S PERFORMANCE

The traditional yardstick for measuring salesmen's performance is sales volume. The salesman who sold more was considered to be better than the one who sold less. This is still so today in very many companies. Sales volume is the only yardstick used.

As indicated in other parts of this book, sales volume, by itself, is a very poor measure of the performance of salesmen. For one thing, it directs their attention to maximizing sales, which is usually accomplished by concentrating selling effort on the products that are the easiest to sell, but which may not be the most profitable from the company's point of view. The other is that many other factors beyond the salesman's control influence the volume of sales. If the evaluation of performance is to be realistic and fair, then only those elements of the job which are within their control should be included in the appraisal.

The purpose of the appraisal is to identify areas of weakness so that corrective action can be taken to ensure that targets will be achieved and that overall performance conforms to the standards laid down. It should be used to identify specific training needs in particular, and in general to rate the individual's overall performance.

| | |
|---|---|
| Excellent | Fair |
| Very Good | Poor |
| Good | Very Poor |
| Average | |

in order to decide

promotion, either in position or pay;
transfer to another job;
termination of employment.

The two instruments for evaluating performance are the job specification and the man profile. Some of the elements making up the job and the profile of the man are capable of more or less objective measurement. In many cases, however, the assessment can only be subjective, and it is essential that it be impartial. The value of breaking down the job specification and the man profile into their elements is that we can get a much more detailed and thus more useful, overall picture of the individual's performance, instead of having to rely on a vague general impression.

In the case of those elements which can only be assessed subjectively and you are using the Excellent, Very Good, Good, Average, Fair, Poor, Very Poor rating scale, ensure that you have defined exactly what you mean in each case. In general, they can be defined as follows:

*Excellent*. Exceptionally high standard of work which leaves little or nothing to be desired. Very few individuals will qualify for this as an overall rating of performance in most organizations. Such a person requires little or no supervision and the manager can depend upon him completely.

*Very Good*. Generally high-quality performance, with sound judgement and mastery of the job. Such people regularly contribute more than is demanded of them.

*Good*. A standard of performance which indicates thorough attention to and accomplishment of all responsibilities and duties. Problems and difficulties are generally handled well, and he strives to improve his performance. His contribution is usually more than demanded.

*Average*. Performs his assigned duties well, but requires supervision. Does not go out of his way to contribute more than demanded of him.

*Fair*. A standard of performance which is adequate for the job. Competent, but requires close supervision and training.

*Poor*. Marginal performance, considerable improvement required.

*Very Poor*. Incompetent, even under supervision. Improvement probably impossible.

If you have done your selection properly, the overall ratings of your salesmen should be between Excellent to Fair. Usually the number who qualify for an overall rating of Excellent will be less than 5%, and most of them should be Average or above. The only people who should qualify for a Fair rating are trainees. Ideally you should have no one with an overall rating of Poor or Very Poor, and if you do you will have to consider terminating their employment. Ratings for the individual elements of performance can be right across the scale, and even your best men will rate poorly on some of them. You will be able to tell where closer supervision, training or counselling are required.

## EVALUATING PERFORMANCE AGAINST THE JOB SPECIFICATION

### 1. *The Objectives of the Job*

Does he understand them; does he agree with them; is he committed to them?

### 2. *Quantitative Sales Targets*

By itself, as a single total figure, a target sales volume is useless. Detailed quantitative sales targets broken down by:

areas,

individual customers or customer classification,

new customers,

individual products or product groups,

the number of orders expected,

the average size of orders expected,

by units and value,

on the other hand, are very valuable for two reasons. Although they should not be used as the only measures of the salesmen's performance, since so much lies outside their control, they may be used in conjunction with all the other individual element ratings to give an overall assessment of performance. The review of results may also reveal weaknesses, or suggest changes in, your sales policy.

What we are doing, when we give these targets to salesmen, in effect, is to say: "With a given product, of a given quality, at a given price, with a given level of advertising and promotion, and other specified support; and with as accurate an assessment as possible of economic and competitive conditions; we believe that these targets are achievable if, in addition, you perform your job as it is specified."

Study of the variances between the targets and achievement will reveal the likely causes. If the causes are obviously beyond the control of the individual salesman, no blame can be attached to him. The study of the causes beyond the salesmen's control will help you in the review of your whole marketing and sales policies. The study of the causes within the individual salesman's control will enable you to decide which aspects of his performance need to be improved.

### 3. *Work Loads*

Provided that the work loads have been accurately measured in the first place and an agreed reasonable target for the number of calls has been established, then the salesmen are fully accountable for their achievement. If they are not being achieved, then help and training in the planning aspects of the job is probably required. If there is a consistent short-fall in achievement, it may be necessary to restudy the job and the territories.

### 4. *Knowledge*

What knowledge of the company, its products, markets and competitors is required by the salesmen? Having specified what is required, the level of knowledge possessed can be assessed either by direct observation, or better still, by suitably structured questionnaires. Generally speaking, salesmen are given insufficient information about the company. So far as product knowledge is concerned they are often given too much of the wrong sort. The kind of product knowledge they do need is information that is of interest to the customer, and technical information only in so far as it is required to substantiate the claims made for the product. Quite frequently the salesmen are left to find out about the company's markets and competitor's activities by themselves. Whilst salesmen's reports in these areas are extremely important, the company should not rely entirely upon this source of information.

### 5. *Attitudes*

Does he really understand the necessity for selling in a free economy? Has he the will to succeed in a selling career—or does he secretly believe that a sales job is only a third-rate occupation?

Again, attitudes can be tested by questionnaire. If you are going to rely on direct observation, be very careful. Your opinion about his attitudes should be built up over a considerable period of time, and it is all too easy to get the wrong impression. The difficult person who is always asking awkward questions usually does so because he is seeking reassurance, not just to be a nuisance.

### 6. *Planning*

Does he plan his journeys and the content of individual calls and, if so, how well? This is an area where vast improvements can usually be made. Most salesmen are poor in the planning aspects of their jobs. Maybe it is the fault of their sales managers, but they seem to think that unless they are constantly dashing around they are not really working. Their work would be more effective in fact, if they spent one, or even two, days at home once a month, planning their next month's work.

### 7. *The Selling Process*

You will have to gauge how well he performs in the actual sales interview by personal observation.

Does he overcome obstacles to the interview or is he easily put off?

Is the person he sees the real decision-maker?

How does he open the sales interview? Does he gain the customer's attention and arouse interest by identifying the customer's main problems or buying interests in respect of the product or service he is selling?

How well does he present the case for buying? Does he create desire in the customer's mind by satisfying those problems or interests with appropriate solutions, benefits and advantages?

Does he anticipate, overcome and capitalize upon objections to a sale?

How does he close the interview? Does he ask for the order— or if his job is such that orders are not placed then and there, does he get a commitment of some sort from the customer?

How does he handle complaints?

Does he keep the customer sold? Is he always a welcome visitor? Is he getting the right share of the customer's business?

Many sales training programmes concentrate almost entirely on this aspect of the sales task, but the other aspects should receive equal attention.

## 8. *Reports*

What reports are essential? How well does he write them? Are they clear and informative? Most salesmen hate report writing, so it is best if you can keep this down to an essential minimum.

## 9. *Self-development*

Apart from formal training, does he continually strive to do better?

The standard of performance of all the other occasional elements of the sales task can be assessed in a similar manner.

## EVALUATING PERFORMANCE AGAINST THE MAN PROFILE

The salesman should also be rated against the man profile. Many of the factors will change naturally in the course of time and others are capable of being changed to bring them closer to the ideal.

## Qualifications

### 1. *Age*

Obviously the individual will grow older, and your company may have an "up or out" policy with regard to age, like the Armed Services.

### 2. *Education*

Whatever their full or part-time education was before you employed them you can do nothing about of course. But their general education can be extended by part-time study. This may be desirable, particularly in the case of the younger men, if their educational achievements are not as high as they should be.

### 3. *Marital Status*

A single man will probably want to get married sooner or later and this will usually limit his mobility. So if great mobility is essential for the job, then you will have to find him another one.

### 4. *Health*

Unfortunately good health cannot be guaranteed for ever, and therefore this should be checked occasionally.

### 5. *Interests*

Over a period of time, a man's outside interests may grow to the point that they start to interfere with his work.

### 6. *Experience*

This is growing all the time.

### 7. *Location*

If you have to redesign territories, the locations of the salesmen's homes may no longer be appropriate.

**Personal Qualities**

The assessment of these factors is very subjective, but it is possible to make some assessment of them and thus the direction in which change may be desirable and achievable by training. Some changes may be achieved quickly, others slowly, and some not at all.

### EVALUATION OF TRAINING

Having completed the evaluation of performance you should now be in a position to set targets for specific improvements in specific areas in a specific period of time during which training will take place, for the sales force as a whole and for the salesmen individually. At your next regular evaluation of performance you will then be able to see what improvements have been achieved as a result of training.

### REVIEW OF OBJECTIVES AND STRATEGY

This system of management is not a static concept, but a continuous dynamic process.

The information gained from the evaluation of the performance of all the activities within the company becomes, in turn, an input for the next cycle of:

> Discovery and Research
> Formulation of Policy
> Planning
> Implementation
> Control

Thus, the evaluation of the performance of the sales force becomes, along with all the data derived from your research activities, the basis for the review and reformulation of your sales objectives and strategy, which in turn will require revised plans, implementation and control.

This brings us back to where we started; the circle is complete.

# CHAPTER 8

# WAREHOUSING AND DISTRIBUTION

MANY sales managers will find themselves responsible for depots or warehouses and their associated distributive systems. Although they will probably not be concerned with the details or actual operations, they should be conversant with the principles of warehousing and distribution management.

## STOCK MANAGEMENT

### What is a Stock?

A stock may be defined as a buffer or shock absorber to even out the differences or discontinuities between supply and demand along a channel of distribution. For example:

$\downarrow$
Factory Raw Material Stock
$\downarrow$
Factory Work in Progress Stock
$\downarrow$
Factory Sales Warehouse
$\downarrow$
Wholesale Warehouse
$\downarrow$
Retail Stockroom
$\downarrow$
Retail Showroom
$\downarrow$
Consumer Stock (Larder)
$\downarrow$
Consumer

At each stage along the channel of distribution, supply will never exactly match the demand. Each stock is thus a reservoir that can accept a variety of supply inputs—to facilitate economic production—and convert them to a different set of outputs—to meet demand.

A water reservoir is a good example of a stock of a single product. Demand for water is fairly constant, but increases in hot weather. Supply of water (rain) is intermittent, and negligible in hot weather. The reservoir is the buffer between the two, thus making it possible for a continuous and sometimes excessive demand for water to be adequately served by an intermittent and sometimes negligible supply.

A stock, therefore, provides an essential economic service between consumer and producer. A stock-keeping operation is not parasitical—it does not just add unnecessary costs to the distribution process by separating the consumer from the producer.

### The Objectives of Stock Management

Stock management is an integral part of business management, it is not just a technique which might be useful in certain businesses, but not in others. Every factory has several different types of stock—raw materials, work in progress, finished goods—but stock-keeping, as such, is the business of any wholesaler or retailer.

The objectives of stock management is to provide a competitive service to meet demand at minimum cost.

### The Importance of Stock Management

Overstocking, to meet all possible (and impossible) demands, causes excessive operating costs, ties up capital, uses valuable space, etc., and thus impairs profitability.

Most stores, both distributive and manufacturing, are over-stocked. The extent of overstocking is of gigantic proportions. So vast indeed, that it is one of the contributory causes of the country's economic weakness. Proper stock management could solve many of our economic problems.

Another danger of overstocking is that a small change in demand is not transmitted through the distributive channels quickly enough to alert producers to alter production accordingly. A small change in demand at the consumer end has a snowballing effect along the distributive channels and can cause boom or bust conditions at the raw material extraction and manufacturing end.

A small decline in the demand for motor-cars, for instance, could thus possibly cause a major economic recession. People in the motor industry would be thrown out of work, thus causing demand to slacken in other sections of the economy, throwing more people out of work, and so on, and so on.

The disadvantages of understocking are equally obvious. A stock-out in a factory can bring the whole organization to a standstill. In wholesale or retail operations, the consequence might not be so drastic, but customer goodwill can be impaired.

So far as wholesalers and retailers are concerned, stock management is the essence of the business. Whether the operation makes a loss, a bare living, or a handsome profit, depends on how good the stock management is.

### The Stock Model

The fluctuation in the stock level of any item can be illustrated as shown in Fig. 8.1.

In order to demonstrate the principle, it has been assumed that the rate of demand is constant. Due to the demand, stock levels fall until the predetermined reorder stock level or review time is reached. A new order is placed but the stock level continues to fall until the quantity ordered is received. The interval of time between the placing of the order and receiving the goods is called the Lead Time or replenishment period. Stocks then rise to a maximum and are then depleted again due to the demand. The cycle is repeated and the saw-tooth diagram results.

Reorder Level $(g)$. The reorder level of stock is the quantity of stock which would be sold during the longest period of delivery (maximum lead time) from the suppliers, at a time which sales reach the maximum level forecast, i.e.

Reorder Level $(g)$=Max. Dly. Period (days, weeks, months)  ×
Forecast Max. (daily, weekly, monthly) Sales.

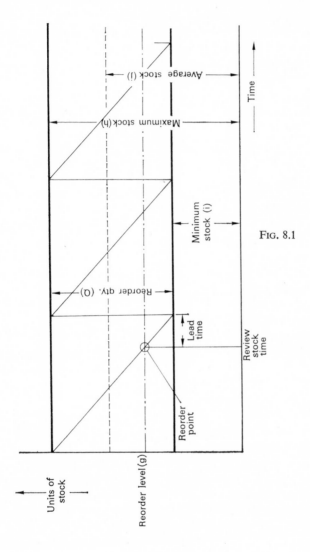

Fig. 8.1

Minimum (or Safety) Stock (*i*). The minimum stock is the level of stock required to meet the worst foreseeable contingencies. It is the Reorder Level (*g*) *less* the quantity of stock that would be sold during a delivery period of average length, at a time when sales are at the average level forecast, i.e.

Minimum Stock (*i*)=Reorder Level (*g*)—(Av. Dly. Period (days, weeks, months) × Forecast Av. (daily, weekly, monthly) Sales).

Maximum Stock (*h*). The maximum stock is the Reorder Level (*g*) *plus* the Reorder Quantity (*Q*) *less* the stock that would be sold during the shortest delivery period, at a time when sales reach the minimum level forecast, i.e.

Maximum Stock (*h*)=Reorder Level (*g*)+Reorder Qty. (*Q*)— (Min. Dly. Period (days, weeks, months) × Forecast Min. (daily, weekly, monthly) Sales).

Average Stock (*j*). The average stock is half the Reorder Quantity (*Q*) plus the Minimum Stock (*i*), i.e.

Average Stock $(j)=\dfrac{\text{Reorder Quantity }(Q)}{2}+\text{Min. Stock }(i).$

Reorder Quantity (*Q*). The simplest way to calculate the Reorder quantity is as follows:

*Q*—Av. Dly. Period × Av. Forecast Sales.

This may be satisfactory in many cases, but it does not take account of the various costs involved.

In order to establish the economic order quantity a balance has to be struck between the cost of holding stock and the cost of ordering. If smaller stocks are held, but more orders placed, the cost of holding stock will be lower and the turnover correspondingly higher, but the cost of ordering will also be higher.

The relationship can be shown graphically as in Fig. 8.2.

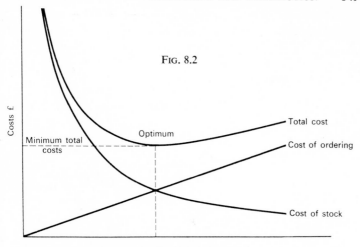

Fig. 8.2

There are various ways of calculating the economic order quantity. Operational researchers have devised a number of models or formulae, and a simple example is as follows:

$$Q = \sqrt{\frac{(2 \times C \times b)}{(P \times I) + (2 \times A \times S)}}$$

where $Q$ = economic order quantity,

$b$ = average sales over the period (week, month, year),

$C$ = total cost of preparing one purchase order,

$P$ = cost price of one unit (including carriage in),

$I$ = required rate of return on capital employed over the period (week, month, year),

$A$ = storage area of one unit,

$S$ = cost of 1 ft² of storage space.

This formula will apply in many cases, but there are situations in which there will be another solution:

(a) When space is of prime importance, then the order quantity would not be "economic" but could be:

$$\text{Order Quantity} = \frac{\text{ft}^2 \text{ allocated for this type of stock}}{\text{ft}^2 \text{ per unit}}$$

TABLE 8.1

| 1. Forecast annual sales (b)<br>2. Cost of purchase order (C)<br>3. Required return on capital (I). | 4. Unit storage area (A)<br>5. Cost of one sq. ft. (S)<br>6. Weight of unit | | 7. Material descripton/code<br>8. Location ---------<br>9. Minimum stock (i) | |
|---|---|---|---|---|
| | Number of orders placed per annum | | | |
| | 1 | 2 | 4 | 12 | 52 |
| 10. Order quantity (Q) | b | b/2 | b/4 | b/12 | b/52 |
| 11. Average stock $(j = \frac{Q}{2} + i)$ | High | | | | Low |
| 12. Cost per unit $(P_1)$ | Constant | | | | |
| 13. Inwards delivery cost $(P_2)$ (incl. internal handling) | Low | | | | High |
| 14. Discounts receivable $(P_3)$ | High | | | | Low |
| 15. Estimate of spoilage/waste (W) | High | | | | Low |
| 16. Annual cost of purchases $(=bxP_1)$ | Constant | | | | |
| 17. Annual cost of inwards delivery $(=bxP_2)$ | Low | | | | High |
| 18. Annual total of discounts $(=bxP_3)$ | High | | | | Low |
| 19. Annual cost of waste $(=bxW)$ | High | | | | Low |
| 20. Annual cost of purchasing $(=Cx$ no. of orders) | Low | | | | High |
| 21. Annual cost of storage $(=jxAxS)$ | High | | | | Low |
| 22. Annual cost of capital $(=(P_1 + P_2 - P_3 + W) \times jxI)$ | High | | | | Low |
| 23. Total cost<br>24. Economic order quantity equals lowest total cost | | | | | |

(b) Where shelf life is important, then:
   Order Quantity = Forecast Sales per day × Shelf Life in days. In this case it is doubly important that the oldest stock is cleared first, using the principle of First In—First Out.

(c) Items in short supply or on allocation from suppliers.

A more accurate, but tedious, method of calculation is as shown in Table 8.1.

**Information Required for Stock Management**

The starting-point of stock management is to get the facts. The information required falls broadly into three categories:

(i) *Analysis of demand*

Who are the customers and what are they buying?

Which products or groups of products are:

| | |
|---|---|
| turning over rapidly | (if retail or wholesale, promote these)? |
| basic demand lines | (retain)? |
| slow sellers | (consider eliminating)? |
| not moving at all | (eliminate)? |

Should any additions to the range be made?
What are the long-term trends in sales?
What are the seasonal patterns of sales?

(ii) *Analysis of supply*

This information is required to decide upon the best suppliers for price, range, speed and frequency of delivery, dependability, and credit terms. The information thus obtained from (i) and (ii) above can then be used to calculate:

the quantity of each product to hold in stock,
when and how much to order.

(iii) *Analysis of the existing store operation*

This is required to see where improvement in layout, documentation and handling can be made in line with the information obtained from (i) and (ii) above.

Collecting all this information can be a large and difficult job, especially if records are not readily available. Supplier's invoices and your own copy invoices will provide most of the information required if no other records exist. The job is, however, not quite so difficult as it first appears. It is a fact that in most businesses only 20% of the products in a range account for 80% of the sales. Therefore, if 1000 products are held in stock it is only necessary, initially, to deal with 200 of them. It is also a fact that about 50% of the products will account for only 3% of sales.

Therefore many of these can be cleared at once without impairing service, goodwill or range of choice. Dead stock should be cleared ruthlessly because it is occupying valuable space.

The job can be further facilitated by drawing up a programme to deal with different groups of related products over a period of time, starting with the best sellers and obvious slow or non-sellers first.

Compile a catalogue of all the products carried under the following headings:

1. *Code number and description*

2. *Demand:*
   (i) Selling price and mark-up ($\%$) per unit of storage.
   (ii) Date and quantity of last sale.
   (iii) Main customers (if any) for line if it is of a specialized nature.
   (iv) Daily/Weekly/Monthly sales (maximum, average and minimum).
   (v) Trend of sales—up or down.

3. *Supply:*
   (i) Suppliers (main and subsidiary).
   (ii) Other products supplied (cross reference).
   (iii) Purchase price and mark-up ($\%$) per unit of storage.
   (iv) Terms, discounts, etc. (cross reference).
   (v) Delivery period from date of order to receipt into stores (maximum, average and minimum).
   (vi) Average quantity received from supplier, irrespective of quantity ordered.
   (vii) Inwards delivery costs (if any).
   (viii) Returnable containers (if any).

4. *Existing store operation:*
   (i) Location in store.
   (ii) Unit of storage (tons, cwt, gross, doz, etc.).
   (iii) Area occupied by one unit of storage.
   (iv) Shelf life if liable to deterioration.

## Stock Classification

1. In many cases it may be adequate to use the stock location reference as a stock number,

$$\text{e.g.} \quad \frac{\text{Store}}{\text{Room 1}} \quad \frac{\text{Row}}{\text{K}} \quad \frac{\text{Bin}}{10} = 1\text{K}10$$

2. Stock number which indicates type of stock. This should be used if the system is mechanized or being run by computer.

| ITEM | | CODE | SIZE | CODE | BRAND | CODE |
|---|---|---|---|---|---|---|
| Canned Beans | | 1 | 10  oz | 1 | Smith's | 1 |
| ,, | Peas | 2 | 16  oz | 2 | Brown's | 2 |
| ,, | Carrots | 3 | $2\frac{1}{2}$ lb | 3 | County | 3 |
| ,, | Beetroot | 4 | 6  lb | 4 | Kent | 4 |

i.e. Beans $2\frac{1}{2}$ lb. Kent = 134
Carrots 10 oz. Brown's = 312

3. Army system.

e.g. Bulb Electric    100 W
Bulb Electric    80 W

## Sales Forecasting

An essential requirement of stock management is a sales forecast of some kind.

The likely future maximum, average and minimum sales are required in order to calculate the stock levels and economic order quantity of each product.

At the very least, the simple arithmetic average of past sales, modified if necessary by experience and knowledge of the business, should be used as a forecast for sales in the period ahead.

## Control Documentation

There are literally hundreds of control documentation systems available. They have been developed by specialist firms in stock control, management consultants, stationery manufacturers, and individual firms for their own use. They range from very simple manual systems to highly complex computerized ones.

The essence of a good stock control documentation system is that it should provide all the necessary information for stock management readily, and in an easily understandable and usable form. It cannot manage stocks by itself. The three vital pieces of information are:

How much to reorder   (Economic Order Quantity—$Q$)
When to reorder        (Reorder Level—$g$)
How much to stock      (Average stock—$j$)

The information necessary to calculate these three figures is obtained from:

*Sales.* Are they increasing, steady or decreasing?
*Costs.* Operating costs and cost of stock.
*Deliveries.* Are delivery times increasing, steady or decreasing, and how frequent are they?

Two typical control documents are shown at the end of this section (Tables 8.2 and 8.3).

The Stock Control Form, which should be kept in the same location as the stock itself, shows all the necessary information relating to sales and deliveries.

The Master Data Card contains all the necessary information relating to costs, the analysis of sales and deliveries, and the calculation of the economic order quantity, reorder level, maximum, minimum and average stocks.

In addition to records for each individual line a summary, by value, of total sales, stocks in hand and on order, and goods received, should be kept. This will give a clear picture of how the business is doing as a whole.


### The Pay-off

The pay-off, in short, is more profit. Other benefits, which in total give increased profits, are:

Better customer service—increased goodwill.
The right levels of stocks to meet demand—no overstocking, no stock-outs.

**Stock Control Form**

Description:

Storage Unit:

Suppliers:

Code No.:

Cross Ref. Code Nos.:

Location:

Terms:

| Week No. | Goods Received | Sales | Moving Average Sales (b) | Stocks | | | Order placed | Notes |
|---|---|---|---|---|---|---|---|---|
| | | | | In hand | On order | Total | | |
| 1. | | | | | | | | Reorder Level = |
| 2. | | | | | | | | Reorder Quantity = |
| 3. | | | | | | | | |
| 4. | | | | | | | | |
| 5. | | | | | | | | |
| 6. | | | | | | | | |
| 7. | | | | | | | | |
| 8. | | | | | | | | |
| 9. | | | | | | | | |
| 10. | | | | | | | | |
| 11. | | | | | | | | |
| 12. | | | | | | | | |
| 13. | | | | | | | | |
| 14. | | | | | | | | |
| 15. | | | | | | | | |
| 16. | | | | | | | | |
| 17. | | | | | | | | |
| 18. | | | | | | | | |
| 19. | | | | | | | | |
| 20. | | | | | | | | |
| 21. | | | | | | | | |
| 22. | | | | | | | | |
| 23. | | | | | | | | |
| 24. | | | | | | | | |
| etc. | | | | | | | | |

TABLE 8.3

## Master Data Card

Description:
Storage Unit:
Suppliers:

Location:

Code No.:
Cross Ref. Code Nos.:
Terms:

| Cost of One Purchase Order: £ (C) | Cost of 1 sq. ft. of Storage: £ per week (S) | Storage Area per Unit: sq. ft. (A) | Required Return on Capital: % per week (I) |
|---|---|---|---|

| Week No. | Forecast Weekly Sales | | | Cost Price per unit (P) | Econ. Order Quantity $Q = \sqrt{\dfrac{2Cb}{PI+2AS}}$ | Selling Price per unit | Delivery Period in weeks | | | Reorder Level $g = ad$ | Maximum Stock $h = g + Q - cf$ | Minimum Stock $i = g - be$ | Average Stock $j = \dfrac{Q}{2} + i$ |
|---|---|---|---|---|---|---|---|---|---|---|---|---|---|
| | Max. $a$ | Ave. $b$ | Min. $c$ | | | | Max. $d$ | Ave. $e$ | Min. $f$ | | | | |

Note: Since all the figures are constants except (b), re-calculation of $Q$ is simplified by calculating $\sqrt{(2C)/(PI + 2AS)}$ to find the constant factor. Multiply this factor by $\sqrt{b}$ for every new value of $b$.

The right range to meet demand—minimum of slow sellers, no dead stock.

Higher turnover.

Less capital tied-up.

More space.

Less effort, in the long run.

## DISTRIBUTION MANAGEMENT

### Introduction

Physical distribution is an integral part of the marketing process. Hitherto it has been rather a neglected field of study, but today it is recognized as being just as important as the other individual components in the marketing mix. This new awareness has come about for two reasons:

(i) The very high costs of storage and transport. In the case of fast turnover consumable goods—such as fresh vegetables—the cost of distribution may be as much as four times the cost of production.

(ii) A company's physical distribution policy is a major strategic competitive weapon.

The objective in physical distribution management is to provide a competitive standard of service to the customer at minimum *total* cost. Costs must be viewed as a whole, because a reduction in one area may produce a more than proportionate increase in another. For instance, it may be cheaper overall to employ an expensive means of transport, such as air freight, because this eliminates the need for local depots and stocks, and associated management problems, which in total may be very much more expensive.

Physical distribution decisions fall into three main areas:

(i) Channels.

(ii) Number and location of depots.

(iii) Transportation.

**Information Required**

The starting-point, as in all areas of management generally, is to get the facts. The information required for physical distribution decisions is similar to that required for planning the marketing mix as a whole and the individual component media in particular, namely, the product itself, pricing, sales force, advertising, sales promotion and public relations. And it will be derived from the same source—market research.

Specifically you will want to know:

1.  *The market*
    Size of market?
    Volume in units and value?
    Own and competitors' shares?
    Who are the customers?
    Where are they located geographically?
    What are their buying habits and preferences?
    What is the frequency of purchase?
    What is the average size of each order?

2.  *The product*
    Unit value
    Bulk
    Perishability
    Service requirements
    Substitutability
    Seasonality

3.  *Competitors*
    Who are they?
    Current policies and practices
    Strengths and weaknesses

4.  *Intermediaries/middlemen*
    Number
    Size
    Location
    Current policies and practices
    Strengths and weaknesses

5. *The company*

> Human, material and financial resources in general. Availability of depots and transport facilities, either own or hired, in particular.

None of these factors are constant, but change with time, some more rapidly than others.


## Channels

The selection of the appropriate channel(s) of distribution will depend upon the factors listed above in general, the customer interface—that is, all the people who have to be influenced to get the product into use or consumption—in particular, and the channels available. In general, intermediaries or middlemen should be used when considerations of cost outweigh the desirability of tight control over each stage in the distribution system.

Changes are continually taking place in the distributive pattern. In recent years we have seen the growth of the retail multiples and voluntary groups, and in industry, vertical, horizontal and conglomerate integration. Another development has been the rapid growth of the mail order business.

The trend towards larger buying units in the consumer distributive trades will no doubt continue, and we can expect to see the larger retailers extending their influence down through to the manufacturing end.

On the other hand, manufacturers are likely to seek to gain a tighter control of their marketing effort by vertical integration up towards the retail end.

However, there is a limit to which vertical integration is possible. A three-cornered battle between the producers of wool and cotton, and the manufacturers of synthetic fibres to gain control of the textile and clothing manufacturing industries, and the wholesale and retail distributive trades, for instance, is clearly unthinkable, at least in the foreseeable future.

In practice the number of alternative choices of channels of distribution will be fairly limited in any particular market. The decision will depend on an assessment of the most economic method of achieving marketing objectives, and it should be reviewed periodically in the light of changing conditions.

## Number and Location of Depots

Decisions about the number and location of depots cannot realistically be made in isolation from decisions about transportation. For the sake of simplicity, however, it is assumed here that the means of transport is given.

The objective, as mentioned before, is to provide a competitive standard of service to the customer at total minimum cost.

The number and location of depots will depend upon the location of production in relation to the location of customers. Bulky, low-value articles, or highly perishable goods, will normally be produced in close proximity to the market, possibly impeding large-scale production. High value, smaller products may be distributed from large centralized production units, or they may not. Heavy specialized machinery may be moved long distances due to the localized nature of production, raw material sources and availability of skilled labour.

Numerous variable factors therefore have to be taken into consideration at reaching the optimum solution. However, the number of alternatives, as in the case of deciding upon the appropriate channel(s), is usually quite limited. The problem is usually a matter of optimizing a given situation, rather than trying to achieve a theoretically perfect solution. In many cases, all we can do is to make the best of a bad job.

Customer service is usually defined in terms of the time required to deliver the goods. What the "right" speed and frequency of delivery should be will depend upon the competition. If standards of service err too much on the late side, then not only is customer goodwill likely to be impaired, but also valuable orders may be lost. With a given means of transportation and pattern of customer demand, the standard of service can be improved by having more, but smaller, depots. So a balance has to be struck between the cost of losing business and the cost of retaining it. Most sales managers tend to err on the side of giving too much service to customers and they should be made aware of the cost of doing this.

In addition, the greater the number of depots, the greater the investment in stock must be for a given volume of sales. Furthermore, smaller depots are usually more expensive to operate per unit of throughput than larger ones.

Having decided the optimum number of depots, it is then possible, with a given geographical distribution of customers, a given volume of business, and a given standard of service to choose the optimum location of depots in order to minimize the total cost of transportation. Transport costs will increase in proportion to the distance from each depot, and equal cost boundaries around delivery zones served by each depot can be defined.

Mathematical techniques are available to solve this problem. The calculation requires large amounts of data and the aid of a computer.

Once the depot locations and delivering zones have been established, it is then possible to plan routes and vehicle schedules to make the optimum use of the means of delivery.

## Transportation

The means of transport is part of an integrated system. The choice, therefore, should not, ideally be made in isolation.

However, if:

the geographical distribution of customers,

the volume of business,

the number and location of depots,

and the stock levels in each depot

are given, the choice of the appropriate means of transport will depend upon the comparative costs in relation to a desired standard of customer service.

The faster the speed and frequency of delivery the higher the cost of transport. The slower, the greater the risk of losing business. So again, a balance has to be struck between the costs of losing and retaining business. This may be illustrated graphically as in Fig. 8.3.

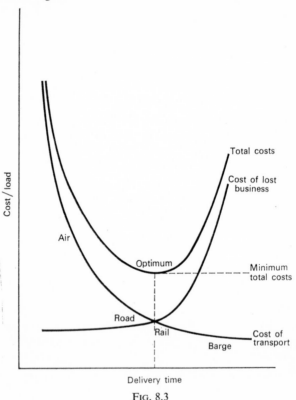

Fig. 8.3

## Own or Hire

The choice of whether to own or hire warehouse space and/or transport facilities may be determined by break-even analysis. The total cost of owning should be compared with the total cost of hiring at different levels of activity. In the case of warehouse space, the cost of storage should be related to the average number of square feet used per year. For transport, the cost should be related to the average number of ton-miles required per year (see Fig. 8.4).

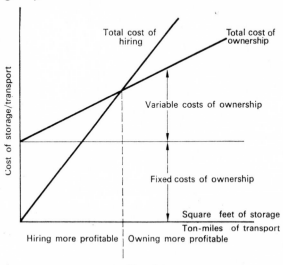

FIG. 8.4

## Integrated Distribution Systems

All the individual elements of the physical distribution system are interdependent. It is therefore possible, in theory to plan, operate and control the system as an integrated whole. In fact, it is possible to conceive of the whole firm as an integrated system of materials flow. That is, from the inwards delivery of raw materials into stock, then into production and work in progress, then to the finished goods warehouse, then transportation into sales depots, and finally transportation to the customers' warehouse.

The planning of a complete integrated system is an extremely complex task in itself. The application is even more difficult, because it is essentially a concept of lateral communications flow across the organization structure, whereas the traditional, and particularly authoritarian, hierarchy of power is vertical. Nevertheless the idea is gaining increasing acceptance. The actual operation and control of such a system has been made possible by the enormous data-processing power of the electronic computer.

## Distribution Cost Analysis

The purpose of analysing distribution costs is to determine the relative profitability of different products, customers, territories, channels of distribution, etc. Having identified the costs, it is then possible to control them so that profitability is retained.

It is usually quite a problem to identify which costs should be included in the analysis, and their method of allocation.

In general, only those costs, both variable and fixed, which can be directly attributed to a particular activity, product, customer, etc., should be included. Arbitrary allocation of general overheads or establishment costs can produce a very misleading picture.

TABLE 8.4. Analysis of Costs by Product

|  | Total (£) | Product A (£) | Product B (£) | Product C (£) |
|---|---|---|---|---|
| Sales | 10,000 | 3000 | 2000 | 5000 |
| Less cost of: |  |  |  |  |
| Materials | 4500 | 1500 | 600 | 2400 |
| Labour | 1500 | 700 | 100 | 700 |
| Gross margin | 4000 | 800 | 1300 | 1900 |
| Less cost of: |  |  |  |  |
| Sales force | 1000 | 300 | 100 | 600 |
| Advertising | 500 | 300 | 100 | 100 |
| Administration | 700 | 200 | 200 | 300 |
| Warehousing | 300 | 150 | 100 | 50 |
| Delivery | 200 | 100 | 50 | 50 |
| Net margin | 1300 | (250) | 750 | 800 |

Table 8.4 shows clearly that product B is the most profitable on a percentage of sales basis, whilst A is unprofitable.

A similar analysis of the costs involved in serving individual customers or types of customer, based upon the quantities taken, can be prepared to show the relative profitability of each. The analysis can further be broken down to determine the profitability of selling different products to different customers.

From such analyses, it is possible to decide whether certain products should be continued or not, or their prices adjusted; or whether alternative distribution methods can be used to serve marginal or unprofitable customers.

**Conclusion**

It is important to remember that all the elements in the physical distribution system are interdependent. The objective is to provide a competitive service at *total* minimum cost.

The total cost of the distribution system

        is equal to

    the total fixed storage cost

        plus

    the total variable storage cost, including inventory

        plus

    the total transportation cost

        plus

    the total cost of lost sales due to delay

The main contribution that the sales or marketing executive can make towards the efficiency of the distribution system, even if he is not directly responsible for it, is to specify the standard of customer service required. This should be the subject of a completely objective appraisal. It will usually be found that customers are more interested in knowing exactly when deliveries will be made, rather than demanding the urgent or impossible all the time.

# CHAPTER 9

# PRICING POLICY

## INTRODUCTION

ONE of the most important risk decisions a businessman has to take is the appropriate price at which to sell his product/service. Pricing policy, as one of the principal means of attaining the objectives of the business, must of course be consistent with them, and also with the other means employed in their attainment. The selling price of the product/service, properly set, provides the funds to pay for all the other activities within the business consistent with the attainment of its objectives, viz. sales turnover, market standing and profitability.

Price is considered from the point of view of the manufacturer of a product or provider of a service. From this viewpoint, all the activities carried on within the business incur costs. Value, and thus price, is decided in the market place. From the point of view of the customer, the price is the cost to him.

Pricing is a matter of judgement. There are no neat formulae for calculating what the "right" price ought to be. In the absence of clearly defined objectives this decision can be no more than an intuitive guess. However, provided that the objectives are clearly defined, the tools of economic, market and cost analysis can serve as valuable aids to judgement in making the decision.

## WHAT IS PRICE?

In economist's terms, price is the money value at which supply will be in equilibrium with demand. From the point of view of the producer or seller, the price of the product/service is the estimated value at which he can dispose of his planned output.

More generally, the price is the bargain struck between buyer and seller. It is the point at which the buyer is satisfied with the value he is receiving in exchange for his money; and the seller is satisfied with the value he is receiving in exchange for his expertise, skill and costs in time and money.

Price is commonly considered as being simply the cash value per unit of the product/service at the point of sale, i.e. the list price. However, from the viewpoints of both buyer and seller, price can have other dimensions which should not be overlooked.

## The Dimensions of Price

List price
Cash discount
Quantity/volume discount
Seasonal discount
Trade discount
Carriage allowance
Trade-in allowance
Advertising/promotion allowance/support
Price guarantee
Quality guarantee
Penalty clauses in contracts
Quantity guarantee
Credit terms
Spot or forward
Other "terms of trade" generally

The value of these other dimensions is not always fully appreciated—they are either "thrown-in" by the seller or taken for granted by the buyer. They are, however, powerful selling tools for the seller, if used judiciously; and serious cost considerations for both buyer and seller alike.

Considerable care should be taken in manipulating these various dimensions because customers, competitors, and other parties, such as government, can react irrationally to alterations in the price structure. Changes in "price", i.e. list price, may be seen as "fair" or "unfair" as the case may be; and likewise changes in the "non-price" dimensions, i.e. terms, discounts, guarantees, etc.

## WHAT IS A PRODUCT/SERVICE?

In deciding upon an appropriate pricing policy the product/service must be defined very carefully; both in the producer's or seller's own terms and in terms of the values—the benefits and advantages—to the buyer.

The specification of a product is comparatively easy; the accurate specification of a service is usually much more difficult. Products or services which differ from each other in any way must be regarded as distinct and separate. Two products or services are alike, only when they are freely interchangeable. Thus, two products which are objectively (i.e. functionally) and subjectively (i.e. aesthetically) identical must be considered different, if one of them has, in addition, any of the dimensions of price mentioned above, such as a quality guarantee, but the other does not.

Products or services, except in the case of certain raw material commodities, are rarely ever objectively or subjectively identical. The difference may be naturally inherent or deliberately created in order to differentiate a particular product from similar ones.

The dimensions which can differentiate similar products—products whose basic objective (or functional) and subjective (or aesthetic) qualities are almost the same—include:

| *Objective dimensions* | *Subjective dimensions* |
|---|---|
| Quality | Quality |
| Design/style | Design/style |
| Efficiency | Colour |
| Reliability | Packaging |
| Running costs | Advertising/promotion |
| Maintenance costs | Reputation/goodwill/brand image |
| Sales service—delivery, etc. | Salesman's personality |
| After sales service—spares, repairs | The price itself |
| Rate of obsolescence | |
| Packaging | |
| Colour | |

Although we know that these dimensions have to be considered in deciding upon a suitable price, we are faced with several difficulties in practice.

1. Many of the words we use to describe these dimensions or "qualities" are imprecise.

2. Some of the objective qualities are capable of precise measurement and evaluation in terms of money—the performance characteristics of a machine tool, for instance.

Many of the objective qualities can only be roughly estimated and the subjective qualities are largely imponderable. Yet we know that in differentiating similar products one from another, the qualities that cannot be precisely measured are frequently as important, and sometimes even more important than those that can.

3. It is sometimes impossible to decide whether a particular quality is either objective or subjective or partly both. Packaging, for example, may be designed either to be functionally protective or aesthetically attractive or both. Colour, usually considered to be a subjective quality, may have a measurable effect, such as a reduction in the number of accidents in a machine shop, because potentially dangerous parts are more clearly visible.

The price itself may sometimes be the key differentiating quality, regardless of all the other qualities. Products or services which may be so differentiated by price alone are those whose other qualities are almost entirely subjective.

Usually, when all the other qualities are similar, the lower price will be perceived by the buyer as being "better value". However, in some cases the reverse of this may be true. A higher price may be perceived as representing "superior quality" and a lower price will be equated with "cheap and nasty". In this category are the so-called luxuries—those that give pleasure or appeal to vanity. Some people buy things simply because they are expensive. This applies equally to industrial products/services where they are being sold on the basis of increased efficiency or savings. The claims will be subject to scepticism or doubt by the buyer, if the price is too low in relation to the savings claimed.

## BASIC PRICING OBJECTIVES

There are five general basic objectives in pricing which have to be considered all together and a compromise agreed as to their relative importance in individual cases.

### 1. To Achieve a Given Target of Profitability

This is usually the most important objective, and it can be expressed either as a return on capital employed or sales turnover.

The target should be expressed quantitatively, i.e. as a percentage. "Maximum profitability in the long term", a commonly used expression, is so vague that it is meaningless.

In deciding the appropriate profitability target, a compromise has to be made with the other objectives.

A very high rate of return (which will not necessarily result from charging a very high price), or the "quick killing", is rarely advisable except in cases of sudden or short-term demands, i.e. fashions and crazes. High profits will inevitably attract the attention of competitors, which is usually undesirable, or other parties, such as government, or trade unions, which is worse.

A less ambitious target is indicated if it is also desirable to maintain or improve market standing or meet or pre-empt competition.

### 2. To Maintain or Improve Market Standing

A compromise usually has to be made between profitability and market standing, or share. There are no really satisfactory guides as to what the ideal relationship should be; it is a matter of judgement. It can be said though that pricing policies which achieve a very high market share at very low level of profitability, or very high level of profitability and only a small market share, will jeopardize the future existence of the business. Notions about what the right levels ought ideally to be can best be judged by making comparisons between firms within the same sector of industry or other similarly organized firms operating in different markets altogether.

### 3. To Pre-empt, Meet or Follow Competition

Apart from deliberate and concerted attempts at price stabilization, there will nearly always be one firm at any particular time who acts as price leader and has a stabilizing effect on prices. This provides an umbrella for all the other firms in the particular industry. When the leader increases prices, all the others follow suit, and likewise when the leader reduces prices. The individual company, unless it is the leader, has little choice in this situation.

### 4. To Differentiate Product or Company Image

Here again, a compromise has to be made with the other objectives. Usually a market can be segmented into a large mass demand at one end, and smaller specialized demands at the other. The two parts are usually sufficiently distinct so that what may appear to be a small or even minute share of the total market, is nevertheless a worthwhile and profitable share of the specialized sector. Thus price can be used to project the appropriate image—either the "value for money" image in the mass sector, or the "quality and exclusiveness" image in the specialized sector.

### 5. To Achieve Stabilization of Price

Much emotional energy is consumed in any discussion about price stabilization. Some measure of stability is always desirable from the seller's and the buyer's points of view. Instability confuses the buyer and may induce in him a "wait and see" attitude so that his decision is postponed indefinitely. Price stability for the seller is open to much argument—chiefly about the degree of stability desirable and the means of achieving it.

It is generally agreed that, because slight fluctuations in consumer/user demand are magnified at each stage as they are transmitted through the channels of distribution, price stabilization is highly desirable, if not essential, at the raw material extraction and basic commodity end of the pipeline. Without some measure of protection, primary producers are likely to become so discouraged that, even if they are not forced out of business, they withdraw voluntarily. The means of stabilization adopted by primary producers include semi-official co-operatives, marketing boards, etc., which may or may not be subsidized by government, and, of course, "gentlemen's agreements".

At, and near, the consumer/user end of the distributive system, the weight of opinion favours more competition and less stability.

All these objectives apply equally in consumer and industrial markets.

### THE DEMAND CURVE AND ELASTICITY OF DEMAND

Two useful economic concepts are those of the demand curve and elasticity of demand (see Fig. 9.1 and Table 9).

These concepts represent an attempt to quantify our knowledge or assumptions about human behaviour. Economists have determined a number of elasticities and, in so far as they assist us in visualizing the interaction of the underlying forces, are useful aids to judgement in pricing decisions.

Three elasticities are of particular importance. Price elasticity is concerned with the change in the quantity of a product/service demanded as a result of a change in price. Income elasticity is concerned with the change in the quantity demanded as a result of a change in income. Cross elasticity is concerned with the change in the quantity demanded of a particular product when the price of a similar competing product is changed. The notion of elasticity may also be applied to relate the change in quantity demanded as a result of a change in the other "non-price" dimensions of price and the "quality" dimensions of the product/service, mentioned above.

When a change in one of the other factors results in a less than proportionate change in the quantity demanded, the demand is said to be inelastic. When the change in the quantity demanded is more than proportionate, the demand is said to be elastic. When the change is directly proportionate, the demand is said to have unit elasticity; and when the quantity demanded does not change at all, the demand is said to be completely inelastic.

Thus, in the case of price changes, the demand is inelastic when an increase (or decrease) of one unit in price results in a *less* than proportionate decrease (or increase) in the quantity demanded, such that the total revenue (price × quantity demanded) at the new price is more (or less) than it was at the old price.

The demand is elastic when an increase (or decrease) of one unit in price results in a *more* than proportionate decrease (or increase) in the quantity demanded, such that the total revenue at the new price is less (or more) than it was at the old price.

TABLE 9.1. Price Elasticity of Demand

|  | Price (£) | Quantity demanded (units) | Revenue (£) |
|---|---|---|---|
| Inelastic | 10 | 500 | 5000 |
|  | 20 | 400 | 8000 |
| Elastic | 10 | 1800 | 18,000 |
|  | 20 | 600 | 12,000 |
| Unit Elasticity | 10 | 1000 | 10,000 |
|  | 20 | 500 | 10,000 |
| Zero Elasticity | 10 | 750 | 7500 |
|  | 20 | 750 | 15,000 |

The elasticity will, in fact, vary over a range of prices and sometimes the demand curve may show irregularities at certain "psychological" price levels.

These tools of economic analysis are, however, of limited practical help in deciding upon an appropriate selling price. In practice it is virtually impossible to establish the dimensions of demand and they are constantly changing. At best, we can only

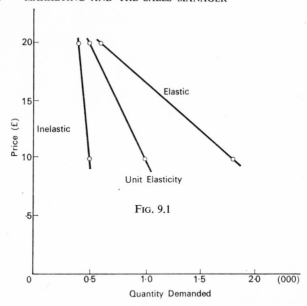

Fig. 9.1

make rough assumptions (guesstimates) about the nature of demand and its sensitivity to changes in the economy generally and in price, income, quality, advertising, competition, sales force activity, speed and frequency of delivery, etc., in particular. Underlying these concepts is the whole diversity and complexity of human and, thus, market behaviour. Pricing decisions must, therefore, be based upon a sound analysis of market behaviour in any particular set of circumstances.

Formal market research can help greatly in providing a better understanding of the underlying forces at work in the market. In the absence of market research, formal or informal, experience based upon years of observation may be the only guide.

## ECONOMIC AND MARKET CONSIDERATIONS

Pricing decisions must be based upon a sound analysis of the behaviour of the economy generally and the market sector concerned in particular. The more formal the approach to the analysis and interpretation of the data, the better, even if it is not dignified as a discrete Market Research & Forecasting function within the company.

Briefly, factors to consider include:

1. *The general economy.* Long-, medium- and short-term trends can be identified. Long-term trends constitute the "broad stream of history"; medium term involving the business cycle; and short term, such as the seasonal cycles.

Within this general area, the broad changes taking place under the headings listed below should be watched because they will have some effect, directly or indirectly, on the company as a whole and thus some bearing on its pricing policies in particular.

(i) Population.
(ii) Employment and income.
(iii) Consumption and expenditure.
(iv) Distribution, transport and communication.
(v) Production.
(vi) Technology.
(vii) Politics.
(viii) Climate/weather.

2. *The market.* Under this heading should be included:

(i) Products, processes or services in direct or indirect (substitute) competition and their objective and subjective qualities.
(ii) Consumers/users—who may be well or ill-informed, and their requirements—which may be rational or irrational.
(iii) Prices and margins.
(iv) Distributors—whose rationale is different from that of either the manufacturer or eventual consumer/user.
(v) Competitors—direct, indirect and potential—who like the consumers/users and distributors, may be well or ill-informed and whose behaviour may be rational or irrational.

## COSTS IN PRICING

Cost enters into the pricing decision by its influence on the supply side of the supply/demand relationship. In the long term costs govern supply, and selling prices must cover costs.

As a general rule, cost at any particular time represents a resistance point to a reduction in price. In the long term, if reductions in cost do not keep pace with reductions in price, the supply of the particular product/service will be reduced.

Those who wish to be supplied must pay a price that will cover costs, including profit, if the supply is to be maintained. It is usually a problem to decide which costs should be taken into consideration in deciding upon the price. There can be no general rule; each case must be treated individually.

The costs which can be attributed to a particular product/service may be classified into either fixed (costs which are fixed in total and independent of volume produced or sold), or variable (costs which do vary in total depending on the volume produced or sold). In addition, there will be other fixed costs, which are the general establishment costs of being in business, and variable costs which vary with the level of activity of the business as a whole. These costs cannot be directly attributed to any particular product/service, but obviously must be recovered in the long term. Much fruitless argument is caused by trying to apportion these general costs in some arbitrary manner to various products within a range. Some products can be made to appear very profitable and others unprofitable by loading them in varying degrees with costs that cannot be directly attributed to them. However, for the purpose of deciding upon the appropriate price level, only the directly attributable costs need to be considered, since they represent the floor below which the price must not fall. Let us consider as an example product "X". Suppose that we have been able, with the aid of market research, educated judgement and long experience of the business to construct a national demand curve for the product. This demand curve cannot be actually tested in practice, except perhaps in rare cases such as certain branches of a multiple retail chain, which may be operating in conditions that are sufficiently similar to make price the determining factor. It is essentially hypothetical, but it represents a distillation of all our knowledge and experience of the market (see Table 9.2).

TABLE 9.2. Product "X"—Hypothetical Price : Volume Relationship

| Price (1) | Anticipated volume (2) | Revenue $(3) = (1) \times (2)$ |
|---|---|---|
| £ | Units | £ |
| 11 | 600 | 6600 |
| 10 | 740 | 7400 |
| 9 | 910 | 8190 |
| 8 | 1120 | 8960 |
| 7 | 1410 | 9870 |
| 6 | 1800 | 10,800 |
| 5 | 2500 | 12,500 |

Suppose now that we have calculated the directly attributable variable costs—materials, labour, etc.—to be £4 per unit.

TABLE 9.3. Product "X"—Contribution at Different Price Levels

| Price | Anticipated volume | Revenue | Dir. att. var. cost per unit | Total dir. att. var. cost | Contribution to all other overhead costs |
|---|---|---|---|---|---|
| (1) | (2) | $(3) = (1) \times (2)$ | (4) | $(5) = (4) \times (2)$ | $(6) = (3) - (5)$ |
| £ | units | £ | £ | £ | £ |
| 11 | 600 | 6600 | 4 | 2400 | 4200 |
| 10 | 740 | 7400 | 4 | 2960 | 4440 |
| 9 | 910 | 8190 | 4 | 3640 | 4550 |
| 8 | 1120 | 8960 | 4 | 4480 | 4480 |
| 7 | 1410 | 9870 | 4 | 5640 | 4230 |
| 6 | 1800 | 10,800 | 4 | 7200 | 3600 |
| 5 | 2500 | 12,500 | 4 | 10,000 | 2500 |

Table 9.3 shows that a price level of £9 would produce the maximum contribution to all the other overhead costs, including profit. Thus if our principal objective was simply profit, the best

selling price would be £9. However, there are usually other factors to consider.

A good thing cannot be kept secret for long, and a contribution (and the corresponding profit) of this order may attract other potential competitors. Thus, we would have to decide whether to opt for less profit, either at a higher or lower price. A higher price would only be attractive to the small premium conscious sector of the market and still leave the way open for competitors. On the other hand, a lower price might be necessary to meet or pre-empt competition or to achieve a deeper market penetration. Productive capacity, labour and raw materials supply may also be limiting factors.

An entirely different issue arising from this analysis, is that it exposes the fallacy of judging performance, particularly that of salesmen, on turnover alone.

For the sake of completeness Table 9.4 includes the directly attributable fixed costs and surplus to cover all other unattributable costs.

TABLE 9.4

| Price | Antici-pated volume | Revenue | Var. cost per unit | Tot. var. costs | Contri-bution | Dir. att. fixed costs | Surplus |
|-------|------|------|------|------|------|------|------|
| (1) | (2) | (3)=(1) ×(2) | (4) | (5)=(4) ×(2) | (6)=(3) −(5) | (7) | (8)=(6) −(7) |
| £ | Units | £ | £ | £ | £ | £ | £ |
| 11 | 600 | 6600 | 4 | 2400 | 4200 | 1000 | 3200 |
| 10 | 740 | 7400 | 4 | 2960 | 4440 | 1000 | 3440 |
| 9 | 910 | 8190 | 4 | 3640 | 4550 | 1000 | 3550 |
| 8 | 1120 | 8960 | 4 | 4480 | 4480 | 1000 | 3480 |
| 7 | 1410 | 9870 | 4 | 5640 | 4230 | 1000 | 3230 |
| 6 | 1800 | 10,800 | 4 | 7200 | 3600 | *2000 | 1600 |
| 5 | 2500 | 12,500 | 4 | 10,000 | 2500 | *2000 | 500 |

*Say, for additional manufacturing capacity; a new machine, for instance, which would be a direct fixed charge on the product, provided that the machine was only used to make this product and no other.

Clearly, since many of the costs cannot be directly attributed to a particular product, it is impossible to say definitely whether a product is profitable or not, however refined the costing system may be. In the case of a company making a range of products, they can be ranked according to their contributions or surpluses. Provided that the combined surpluses of all the products together are greater than the unattributable costs then the company will make a profit. As another issue, if the products are ranked according to their contributions, it will usually be seen that approximately $20\%$ of them account for approximately $80\%$ of the contribution and some $50\%$ of the products account for only $3\%$ of the contribution. This will give a very clear idea of where some judicious pruning may be done without impairing profitability, service, goodwill or range of choice.

By now it will be apparent that the idea of "cost-plus" pricing, although simple, has little else to recommend it. The fallacy of "cost-plus" pricing is that it completely ignores the demand side of the supply/demand relationship. This fallacy is compounded when the costs to be included and the percentage mark-up are chosen quite arbitrarily.

In actual practice the "cost-plus" price is usually a compromise of the opinions of the various people concerned within the firm and the figures "worked-out" to justify it.

Companies who operate on this system are usually those involved in contracts of one sort or another—mechanical, electrical and civil engineering. An approach, which formalizes this process of setting a price for a contract is as follows. First of all the best estimated cost is worked out, using rigorous estimating techniques, and great care in specifying exactly which costs are to be included or not. Having done this to the satisfaction of all concerned, consideration is then given to the probabilities of winning the contract at a range of prices. The probability figure sums up all the experience and knowledge of the market, the particular customer and competition—of the individuals concerned in making the decision.

The expected profit at each price level is then multiplied by the probability figure to give a weighted "pay-off".

TABLE 9.5. Contract Y
Cost: £10,000

| Price (1) | Profit (2) | Probability (3) | Pay-off (4)=(2)×(3) |
|---|---|---|---|
| £ | £ | | £ |
| 10,000 | 0 ⎫ | | 0 |
| 10,500 | 500 ⎬ | 1·00 | 500 |
| 11,000 | 1000 ⎭ | | 1000 |
| 11,500 | 1500 ⎫ | 0·90 | 1350 |
| 12,000 | 2000 ⎭ | | 1800 |
| 12,500 | 2500 | 0·75 | 1875 |
| 13,000 | 3000 | 0·50 | 1500 |
| 13,500 | 3500 | 0·25 | 945 |
| 14,000 | 4000 | 0·10 | 400 |
| 14,500 | 4500 ⎫ | 0·00 | 0 |
| 15,000 | 5000 ⎭ | | 0 |

Table 9.5 shows that the best profit consistent with the probability of winning the contract will be achieved at a price of £12,500. If the objective is not principally profit, this table also makes more explicit the appropriate price to quote. If the company is short of work then a price with a high probability should be chosen; or alternatively if it has more than enough work on hand then a price with a low probability should be quoted.

## CONCLUSION

Pricing is a vast subject. A company's pricing policy is one of the key marketing tools upon which depends its long-term success.

In establishing a pricing policy, consideration must be given to:

The company's marketing/business objectives—which should be clearly defined—

and a careful analysis of

      customer demand       competition
      distribution       costs.

The pricing strategy must be dynamic and based on a careful analysis of the market conditions at the time. It requires a systematic planned approach consistent with the company's objectives. It is not enough just to pose the questions:

> What do competitors charge?
> What does it cost to make?
> What can we get away with?

# INDEX